LEMON COMPENDIUM

Yasemen Kaner-White

PARMUTO

LEMON COMPENDIUM

Yasemen Kaner-White

CONTENTS

FOREWORD
MAURO COLAGRECO, 2 STAR MICHELIN CHEF (MIRAZUR)

Yasemen Kaner-White's book on lemons is a fascinating and informative read. Her dedicated research and resulting travels have produced a veritable encyclopedia of uses for this sun-drenched and versatile fruit.

As a chef, I have always loved lemon's sheer adaptability in the kitchen. My restaurant Mirazur is situated in the beautiful land of citrus fruit in Menton in South France. I am privileged enough to be able to grow my own lemons in the gardens.

I use them to infuse oils and salt to add subtle bursts of flavour; as a base for thirst-quenching drinks; and juiced, to add rich, palate-cleansing acidity to savoury dishes and clean, palate-lifting freshness to sweet ones. From vegetables, to seafood, meats and desserts, lemon is the perfect partner for any dish.

From an essential culinary ingredient, to a natural antiseptic in household cleaning and even as a useful beauty treatment, Yasemen's *Lemon Compendium* proves just how the uses of lemon can permeate far from the kitchen to encapsulate every room in the home.

This is a book every household should own.

Mauro Colagreco

Mauro created a very special lemony recipe just for Lemon Compendium, which can be found in the Global Grub section, aptly under France, p.184.

INTRODUCTION

The natural question...'Why lemons?' Well the initial inspiration came from living and working within the heady citrus aroma of Cyprus for a few years; with my mixed English and Cypriot heritage attracting my residence. A combination of being surrounded by stunning lemon groves, a love of food, diverse cultures and a thirst for knowledge led me on a path to researching and writing my *Lemon Compendium*. I guess for me, it was a case of 'When life gives you lemons – write a book!'

Luckily lemons are available all year round, though they are at their peak during the summer months. Do not be tempted to buy bottled lemon juice, as nothing is more refreshing and adds that magical touch, than the zesty drops squeezed from the fresh fruit itself. Lemons have been providing both culinary and non-culinary aid from time immemorial. The more I probed and poked around everything and anything to find out as much as I could about the golden fruit that is the lemon and what it has to offer, addictively and gratifyingly, I found there was so much to share. *Lemon Compendium*, is just that, a multifaceted lemon encyclopaedia. This book will take you on a lemony journey, teaching you how to save money, whilst loving the environment by cleaning your house top to toe effectively and organically.

It will guide you on how to treat your body the natural way, both medicinally and cosmetically, as well as providing a priceless tome explaining citrus uses throughout history. You will be able to explore the various types of lemons available worldwide, discover fun things to do with a lemon, such as writing an invisible message with its juice and not forgetting an offering of countless lemonlicious recipes to tingle your taste buds. Enthused by different cultures, I have shared my favourite lemon inspired recipes from around the world, which is reflected in the Global Lemony Grub chapter. Puddings, savoury dishes, drinks; both of the alcoholic and non-alcoholic varieties, can be found in the perhaps more traditional recipe chapters.

It has fascinated me, having spoken with people from around the globe, how the lemon introduces a familiar and unifying topic, one which can be discussed with enthusiasm. Whether it is a lady in Chelsea, London, having lived in India for 20 years, where she noticed the local custom of a single drop of lemon juice being squeezed into the eyes of a newborn, leading her to do the same, every six months, advocating that is why she has such bright eyes and great eyesight at the age of 80, or a Lebanese lady exclaiming that her Father never liked her husband-to-be, so shouted at her to send him a box

of lemons! which was an exaggeration of the saying 'tell them to go suck on a lemon', signalling dislike. She also added that in Lebanon the ladies always mix their tabouleh (delicious local couscous salad) with their hands to act as a moisturiser, due to the olive oil and lemon juice mixture leaving the skin silky soft. Another tale was from a Spanish lady about her neighbour who only uses a cut lemon rubbed under each armpit every morning as an effective deodorant, in preference to some shop-bought deodorants which have been said to contain cancerous properties. A Pakistani lady swears by her home-made remedy for oily skin, of simply equal parts of lemon juice, rosewater and honey, mixed and smoothed on the face, left for 10 minutes and washed away with warm water. In Jerusalem, Israel, the event of Sukkot celebrates local harvests remembering the time when the Israelites trekked through the desert living in temporary shacks. Families build makeshift homes, or sukkot, with open roofs revealing the sky. They live there for seven days, and every day parade around the synagogue with wands made of willow, myrtle, and palm, together with a citron (similar to a lemon) waving them in all directions to honour the gifts from the land, as this is also the Autumn harvest festival. In fact, in many traditions, lemons are commonly used in houses, businesses, cars and on people in an attempt to remove the 'evil eye'.

Although Alfred Newman's quote: 'We are living in a world today where lemonade is made from artificial flavours and furniture polish is made from real lemons' is true for some, this book shows, both lemonade (p.89), furniture polish (p.58) and much, much more can be brought to life naturally, by using the most utilitarian fruit in the world – the lemon. Enjoy!

With lots of lemony love,

Yasemen

LEMON VARIETIES

LEMON & CITRUS VARIATIONS

LEMON – A DICTIONARY DEFINITION

Noun   [1] a pale yellow oval citrus fruit with thick skin and fragrant, acidic juice.
[*mass noun*] a drink made from or flavoured with lemon juice: a port and lemon.

[2] (also lemon tree) the evergreen citrus tree which produces lemons, widely cultivated in warm climates. Citrus limon, family Rutaceae

[3] [*mass noun*] a pale yellow colour: [*as modifier*] : a lemon t-shirt

[4] informal an unsatisfactory or feeble person or thing: car manufacturers cannot afford to create lemons

Derivatives lemony adjective

Origin   Middle English: via Old French 'limon' (in modern French denoting a lime) from Arabic 'līmūn' (a collective term for fruits of this kind)

Etymology   Middle English lymon, from Middle French 'limon', from Medieval Latin 'limon, limo', from Arabic 'laymūn, limūn', from Persian 'līmū, līmun'

Lemon is the worldwide term for both the thorny tree and fruit. The cultivated lemon is believed to be a hybrid of two wild species, most probably lime and citron. Lemon trees can grow to be about 3–7·5m tall, scarcely covered with foliage. The flower has 5 sepals, 5 petals, copious stamens, and 1 pistil. The top of each petal is white, shading to pinkish at the base. Lemon flowers have a sweet aroma, similar but less overwhelming than the fragrance from orange flowers.

Typically, the lemon is a yellow, elliptically shaped berry, which normally has a small nipple-like protuberance at the apex, the end opposite the stem. The exocarp layer is the tough rind, containing oil, which is used in the manufacture of perfumes and lemon flavouring in a whole host of products. The cushiony, white layer beneath the rind is the mesocarp, known as the pith, containing citrin and vitamin P. The pulp, which is the endocarp layer, is made up of 8–10 segments filled with inflated hair cells full of juice, keeping the small, pointed, yellowish seeds moist. Lemons are ancient apomicitic hybrids, meaning their seeds can reproduce without sexual fusion.

The preponderance of cultivated lemon varieties are hybrids producing little true bred seed. Lemon trees are planted into infertile soil, to which fertiliser is frequently added. The rows in lemon groves are planted 6m apart, according to the variety planted, the climate, as well as the topography of the area. Weather permitting, lemons flourish throughout the year. When green and nearly ripe, the fruit is picked from each tree 6–10 times annually and then ripened in warmer conditions. A mature lemon tree can produce up to two thousand lemons per year.

Lemon trees are internationally important beyond the Mediterranean climates to which they are ecologically adapted. They are grown all over the tropical and subtropical regions of the world, primarily in Italy, California, Portugal, and Spain. It has been suggested that lemons were originally brought from the Middle East to Spain and North Africa during the middle ages.

When selecting your lemons, always go for the heavier ones, no matter their size. When juxtaposing two equal sized lemons, the heavier one will most definitely be the richer in sugar and mineral content. Thick skinned lemons are not as heavy as a thin skinned, nor do they have the coveted mineral content or sweetness. Take note of the stem end of the lemon; one end of the fruit has a tip where the blossom started to grow, the other end has a stem or a dimple where the stem used to be. On the stem end of a highly mineralised, sweeter lemon, there will be visible mini lines radiating out of the central point like sunbeams. These lines form a three-to-five pointed star known as the calyx. It has been suggested the greater the number of points on the calyx, the higher the mineral content of the lemon.

Lemon juice is used extensively as a drink, as a constituent of drinks, salad dressings, fish dressings and a flavouring, as demonstrated by this book's ample yummy recipes! Lemon pulp was originally used commercially in the developing of citric acid, and is currently utilised in the making of concentrated lemon juice, which is revered medicinally for its high vitamin C content.

Lemon Compendium will show you countless ways in which to use this amazing fruit to its full potential.

THE TWO EXTREMES: SWEET AND SOUR LEMONS

Sour   The two main types are the *Eureka* and the *Lisbon*. The Eureka generally has more of a textured skin, a short neck at one end and a few seeds, whilst the Lisbon has smoother skin, no neck and is normally seedless.

Sweet   The most renowned sweet lemon is the *Meyer* lemon, a citrus fruit native to China deemed to be a hybrid between a true lemon and either a mandarin or common orange. It was brought to the United States in 1908 by the agriculturalist and explorer Frank Nicholas Meyer, an employee of the United States Department of Agriculture who gathered a sample of the plant on a trip to China. They need more care when shipping and are not widely grown on a commercial basis. However, they withstand the cold better than other lemon varieties and bear fruit, as well as flowers all year round.

LEMON MYRTLE

Botanical Name *Backhousia citriodora*

Myrtle family *Myrtacea*

Backhousia is the botanical name for Lemon Myrtle, assigned to it by Baron Ferdinand von Müller, in 1853, after a nurseryman from Yorkshire named James Backhouse. Lemon Myrtle trees are predominantly grown in Australia, South Africa, and the Southern United States. Of late, the lemon myrtle has been more extensively cultivated in China, Indonesia and Thailand with a view to extracting the essential oil. The Lemon Myrtle shrub is native to Australia, growing prolifically to a height of around 8m in the Queensland rainforest. Its glossy dark green lemon fragrant leaves, resembling bay leaves, grow up to 10cm long. The abundant, large bunches of small white flowers adorn the tips of the branches. Flowers, fruits and leaves are all edible. The lemon myrtle is a common garden plant in Brisbane, but about a million have been planted commercially just for the oil content. The essential ingredient is citral, amounting to over 90% of the plant's essential oil, compared to about 3% oil in the lemon. The oil is extracted by steam distillation.

The leaves are used fresh, dried or ground. The taste is distinctly lemony and tangy, featuring lime and camphor notes. Because the flavour of lemon myrtle is similar to lemon but without the acidity, it is particularly useful in recipes that are dairy based, as it will not curdle. It is unsuitable for using in foods that require lengthy cooking because the lemon flavour dissipates and is replaced with a pungent eucalyptus flavour. Lemon myrtle is thus better suited to flavouring biscuits, ice creams, sorbets, pasta, stir-fries, fish and grilled meat, as opposed to roasts. Lemon myrtle is a great addition to marinades for poultry and fish, flavoured vinegars, salad dressings, and dips. It can be a substitute for lemongrass and suits Asian stir-frys. It can even be used as flavouring in drinks (p.90). Due to the fragile nature of the essential oil, it is important to purchase only small quantities of freshly produced lemon myrtle powder and store in an airtight container in a cool, dark place.

The essential oil found in the leaves (typically 4–5%), consists of terpenoid aldehydes, citral (90–95%), neral and geranial. There are also traces of myrcene, linalool, citronellal, cyclocitral and methyl-heptenone. Citral has a multitude of medicinal uses, containing antimicrobial elements. It features in shampoos, body lotions, soaps, and household cleaners. Since the oil also has insect repellant qualities it is used in pet shampoos to repel fleas. Effective as an antiseptic, it is a herbal remedy for treating gastro-intestinal infections. Its antispasmodic properties aid in alleviating intestinal spasms. Generally, it has a relaxing effect on the body, so throat complaints also can be relieved with this wondrous plant.

VARIETIES OF LEMONS

Armstrong — seedless, also known as Armstrong Seedless. Discovered in 1909, this type of lemon tree can grow up to 6m tall.

Amalphitanum — elongated shape, grows on the Almafi coast of Italy.

Aurantiata — Chinese citron, thought to be a cross between a *Seville* orange and a citron, it is seedless.

Bergamot — (*Citrus Bergamia*) native to Southeast Asia, but now seen mainly in Morocco, Ivory Coast and Italy.

Bernie — a variety grown in Spain.

Bicolore — citron from Lucca, with a skin that is tinged with purple and green until it is fully ripened.

Bush Lemon Tree — naturalised lemon grown wild in sub-tropical Australia. They are very resilient, have a thick skin with a potent lemon flavour and grow to about 4m high in a sunny position. The skin provides excellent zest.

Canaliculata — known for its furrowed outer skin.

Canarone — is known by the deep groove surrounding the protrusion at the bottom of the fruit.

Citrus depressa — intensely sour species, frequently used like a lemon or lime to garnish dishes, also used to make a yellow juice, which can be thinned or sweetened.

Citrus limetta — species of sweet citrus, containing essential oils

Corsican — of Corsican origin and bears sweet fruit.

Diamante — citron named after the city of Diamante, on the South Western coast of Italy, in the region of Calabria. Diamante is probably the best known citron variety.

Digitata — also known as *The Hand of Buddha* due to its appearance, in which each segment is covered by its skin. In the Far East it is seen as a symbol of wealth and happiness, whereas in China and Japan, it is used to fragrance rooms.

Etrog — also called *Israel Citron*, originated in Palestine, where it features in the Hebrew Sukkoth, The Feast of the Tabernacles. The plant sheds its leaves in winter.

Fanatastico — newer and apparently superior bergamot variation, with the oil in its rind being used to flavour Earl Grey Tea. Other variations also include *Castagnaro* and *Feminello*.

Femminello	the most significant lemon group in Italy, growing vehemently and of moderate size at maturity.
Florentina	flowers and bears fruit all year round. Prominent for its delicious juice.
Florentine	citron was collected from the Medici gardens, near Lucca, during the 17th century. The fragrance is highly desirable, the fruit has a prolonged tip.
Foliis Variegatis	features streaky yellow and green leaves. *Foliis Variegatis Sanguineum*, is similar except that its fruit has lengthways striations on the skin.
Imperial	believed to be a lemon and grapefruit hybrid, it is a spiny plant, also called *Lipo* and *Citrus Paradise*.
Kabosu	juicy green citrus fruit, related to the *yuzu* with the tartness of lemon, it replaces vinegar in some Japanese dishes.
Lisbon	bitter with high juice and acid levels. The fruits of *Eureka* and *Lisbon* are very similar. Dynamic and productive, the trees are extremely thorny particularly when young.
Loomi Aswad	(also known as *dried Black Lemon*) a staple pantry ingredient in the UAE. It is actually a key lime and is dried out in the sun and then used whole or in a powder form when cooking stews and mitchboos rice dishes.
Lunario	also known as *Four Seasons Lemon*, it only bears fruit when fully mature, but thereafter very productive.
Maxima	giant citron, with delicious smelling flowers arising in Spring and Autumn.
Otaheite	allegedly from Tahiti, is a cross between a lemon, sweet orange and mandarin. It is renowned for its productiveness and ability to endure low temperatures.
Paradisi	larger than a standard lemon, with the shape of an elongated egg. The tree is very thorny.
Passiflora laurifolia	commonly known as the *water lemon*, is a species in the family *Passifloraceae*. A medium sized, ovaloid fruit, typically green or deep orange skinned, with white to yellow juicy pulp. The *water lemon* has a strong perfumed taste, without the sharpness of the common passion fruit.
Peretta	pear shaped variety cultivated by the Medici in the 17th century.
Perettone	has pear shaped fruit, with long necks. Its leaves shed in winter.
Pigmentata	red lemon celebrated for its excellent fruit.
Ponderosa	also known as *American Wonder* is a citrus species considered to be a hybrid between a lemon and a citron.
Rangpur	also known as lemandarin, is a hybrid between the mandarin orange and the lemon. A citrus fruit with a powerful acidic taste alongside an orange peel and flesh.

Rubra	red citron, with purple buds. When it is ripe, it is orange in colour.
Rugoso	particularly wrinkly citron with light leaves. It flowers twice a year in Spring and Autumn.
Salicifolia	has leaves akin to those of a willow tree.
Salò	originally from Lake Garda.
Sanctus Dominicus	originates from the Dominican Republic, bearing pear shaped fruit, thought to have been grown by Dominican friars.
Sfusato lemon	named due to its pointed ends, *a fuso* means spindle-shaped in Italian.
Shangjuan or Ichang	citrus fruit and plant originating in East Asia. It is considered to be a hybrid of *pomelo* and *Ichang papeda*.
Verna	Spanish variety of unknown origin. It accounts for roughly 60% of Spain's annual lemon crop and is also grown in Algeria and Morocco. It was imported into Australia from Spain, released from plant quarantine in 1994.
Villafranca	imported to Florida by General Stanford.
Volkameriana	thought to be an old hybrid between a lemon and the *Seville* orange.
Yuzuquat	trigeneric hybrid between a *Yuzu* lemon and *Nagami kumquat*, developed by Dr. John Brown in Texas. The fruit is often used as a lemon substitute and is notably seedy.

LEMONS THAT MAKE YOU LAUGH!

Why did the lemon disapprove of his daughter?
Because she was a little tart!

What do you give an injured lemon?
Lemon-aid!

Why did the lemon stop halfway across the road?
He ran out of juice!

What's yellow and wears a mask?
The Lone Lemon!

Watson: Why do you have a yellow door?
Sherlock: Lemon entry my dear Watson!

LEGENDARY LEMONS

LEGENDARY LEMONS

Where lemons are featured within the arts...

BITTER LEMONS BY LAWRENCE DURRELL

Being of mixed English/Cypriot heritage, of course I wanted to mention this book, which naturally I have read sitting under the tree of idleness itself. *Bitter Lemons* is an autobiographical work whereby Durrell depicts in beautifully vivid detail the three years (1953–1956) he spent on the island of Cyprus. The book was awarded the *Duff Cooper Prize* in 1957, the second year the prize was awarded.

As to why the novel is entitled *Bitter Lemons* is up to much debate. It could be because he had a lemon tree in the garden, or perhaps it alludes to the bitter and sweet dynamic of Cypriot lemons which is a reflection of his relationship with the island, also of course, it could be due to Cyprus being scattered all over with the yellow gems, in which case (similar to myself) he would not have had to look hard for inspiration!

LEMON PROVERBS

Interpret as you wish...

Spanish Proverb — *Invite your son-in-law to a fowl, and he will take away the lemon.*

Ukrainian Proverb — *Only when you have eaten a lemon do you appreciate what sugar is.*

Dutch Proverb — *Sell beets/apples as lemons.*

Portuguese Proverb — *If life gives you a lemon, make a caipirinha out of it.*

Maltese Proverb — *A woman is like a lemon; you squeeze her and throw her away.*

American Proverb — *When life hands you lemons, make lemonade.*

Gypsy Proverb — *If you stab out the eye of thy neighbor cut off two fingers and dip them in honey. Cook them in lemon curd and present them to his family in a pigeon pie. If they dine on a full moon his eye will sprout again from its socket.*

Ethiopian Proverb — *Fifty lemons are a load for one person, but for fifty persons they are perfume.*

THE SYMBOL OF A LEMON IN CHRISTIAN ART

Very often symbolised pictures can convey a lot more than words, making religious concepts easily understood when they are used in paintings. A symbol is a means of portraying ideas to the mind via images or pictures. By using repetition, these pictures can become ingrained so that certain images project distinct and well-defined thoughts. The lemon has been said to symbolise fidelity in love, friendship, longevity and purification. It has also been said that a lemon is sometimes shown to allude to the weaning of Christ.

FEATURING LEMONS

The Three Lemons is an old Hungarian fairy tale. The plot revolves around a prince who is determined to find someone to marry before his father passes away.

The Lemon Song was highlighted in the English rock band; Led Zeppelin's 1969 album *Led Zeppelin II*. It was recorded at Mystic Studios in Hollywood when the band was on their second concert tour of the United States. The song is spiked with sexual innuendo and features some of Led Zeppelin's most blues inspired playing.

Lemon is the fourth song and second single from U2's 1993 album, *Zooropa*.

Lemon Jelly is a British electronica duo made up of Nick Franglen and Fred Deakin.

Lemon Tree is a 2008 film, by director Eran Riklis. The film portrays the legal battles of a Palestinian widow to stop the Israeli Defence Minister, her next door neighbour, from uprooting the lemon trees in her family farm. Highly recommended, beautifully shot film.

Lemon Tree is a folk song from the 1960's that was written by Will Holt and popularised by the folk trio Peter, Paul and Mary. It was also sung by Bob Marley.

The Lemon Trees were a 1990's UK pop band.

Lemon Incest translating as 'Inceste de citron', and a wordplay on 'un zeste de citron' (a tang of lemon) is the title of Serge Gainsbourg's song, in duet with his daughter Charlotte Gainsbourg. It demonstrates Serge Gainsbourg's adoration for puns.

Lemon of Troy is an episode of *The Simpsons* featuring the theft of Springfield's Lemon Tree.

The Lemon Tree is an arts venue in Aberdeen, Scotland, managed by *Aberdeen Performing Arts*.

Oranges and Lemons is an English nursery rhyme and singing game which relates to the bells of several churches, all within or near to the City of London. It is listed in the Roud Folk Song Index as #3190.

She Squeezed My Lemon is a 1937 song sung by Roosevelt Sykes.

Orange and Lemons was a Filipino pop rock band formed in 1999. The band's name was initially thought up by a former member of the group. Upon finding out that the name was actually derived from a British nursery rhyme, they changed it to Orange and Lemons.

Lemon Kittens are a post-punk band formed in Reading, Berkshire, England in 1977 by Karl Blake and Gary Thatcher.

The Lemon Pipers were a 1960's psychedelic pop band from Oxford, Ohio, known primarily for their song *Green Tambourine*, which reached No.1 in the United States in 1968.

Lemon Parade is Tonic's first album, released in 1996.

Lemon Sky is a 1988 made for television drama written by Lanford Wilson, based on his play of the same name.

BASToF Lemon is a South Korean animation series, which ran for 26 episodes in 2001.

Oranges & Lemons is a Japanese band formed by the composer-and-performer duo, Masumi Itô and Yôko Ueno.

Gin Lemon is an EP released by Gigi D'Agostino in 1997.

Oranges & Lemons is an album by the British band XTC.

Vodka Lemon is a 2003 film directed by the Kurdish director Hiner Saleem. The story takes place in a Yazidi Kurdish village in Armenia, still suffering economically from the Soviet collapse.

Lemon Love is the debut album recorded by pop singer Aslyn.

Lemons is the third full-length album by singer and songwriter Glen Phillips.

The Lemon Sisters is a 1990 American film from Miramax Films directed by Joyce Chopra and written by Jeremy Pikser.

Bitter Lemon Press is a small London-based independent publisher, set up by Francois von Hurter in 2003 which specialises in translated literary crime novels and roman noir's from abroad.

Dear Lemon Lima is a family comedy feature film written and directed by Suzi Yoonessi, released in 2009. Based on her short film of the same name.

Lemon Tree is a song by German Britpop band Fool's Garden from the album *Dish of the Day*, which was released as a single in 1995 and became a huge international hit in 1996.

Wo die Zitronen blühen (Where the Lemons Blossom) is a waltz by Johann Strauss II written in 1874. The waltz was written during a trip by the composer in Italy where he travelled with the Langenbach Orchestra of Germany and performed the work at the Teatro Regio in Turin on 9 May 1874.

Life Is a Lemon and I Want My Money Back is a radio single by Meat Loaf released in 1994.

The Dog & Lemon Guide of more than 1,000 pages, is said to be the biggest car buyers' guide on earth.

The Lemon Party of Canada (Parti Citron) is a frolicsome Canadian party, which has operated on a federal level, as well as provincially in Quebec.

The Lemon Bay Woman's Club is a notable woman's club in Englewood, Florida, United States. It is located at 51 North Maple Street. On August 11, 1988, it was added to the US National Register of Historic Places.

The drink named for golf legend *Arnold Palmer* is made from combining equal parts lemonade and iced tea: a *"Tom Arnold"* adds vodka, in any quantity, to the mix.

Guinness world records:
The *world's heaviest lemon* weighed 5·265kg on 8 January 2003 and was grown by *Aharon Shemoel* on his farm in Kefar Zeitim, Israel.

The fastest time to peel and eat a lemon is 8·25 seconds, achieved by *Ashrita Furman* at the *Songs of the Soul* offices in New York City, New York, USA, on 3 May 2010.

KENNST DU DAS LAND, WO DIE ZITRONEN BLÜHN? DO YOU KNOW THE LAND WHERE THE LEMONS BLOSSOM?

BY JOHANN WOLFGANG VON GOETHE

'All theory, dear friend, is grey, but the golden tree of life springs ever green'

Goethe, who was born 28th August, 1749 in Frankfurt-on-Main, was a German poet, playwright, novelist, scientist, statesman, theatre director, critic, amateur artist and considered by many to be the greatest literary figure of the modern era. Goethe was inspired to write his celebrated poem 'Do you know the land where the lemons blossom?' upon sailing through Lake Garda and stopping at Limone in September 1786, where he saw the renowned lemon houses. The name of the town Limone Sul Garda, derives from the Latin word Limen, meaning border, though it has been said that it comes from the famed local fruit, the lemon. Limone grew from a typical rural economy based on fishing and olive cultivation, to become the northern area for cultivation of the beautiful fruit, lemon. The inhabitants of Limone built the famed lemon houses, with super-high walls to protect the trees from the North East winds. Limone is allegedly the northernmost place in the entire world which has the ability to grow lemons.

Kennst du das Land, wo die Zitronen blühn,

Im dunkeln Laub die Gold-Orangen glühn,

Ein sanfter Wind vom blauen Himmel weht,

Die Myrte still und hoch der Lorbeer steht?

Kennst du es wohl?

Dahin! Dahin

Möcht ich mit dir, o mein Geliebter, ziehn.

Knowest thou where the lemon blossom grows,

In foliage dark the orange golden glows,

A gentle breeze blows from the azure sky,

Still stands the myrtle, and the laurel, high?

Dost know it well?

'Tis there! 'Tis there

Would I with thee, oh my beloved, fare.

LEMON FESTIVALS AROUND THE WORLD

Who would have thought... So many countries celebrate the miraculous lemon, check out all of these lovely lemon festivals, why not go and visit one or all?

USA: CALIFORNIA: GOLETA

What once began in 1890 with a rancher named Sherman Stow and his 600 acres of lemon groves has slowly transformed into an annual celebration of the iconic fruit that today defines the local region. The California Lemon Festival in Goleta, taking place in October, has become one of the most anticipated annual events in Santa Barbara County. It now attracts close to 35,000 visitors annually, eating their share of 1,720 lemon bars, drinking over 93 gallons of lemon ale, and buying over 932 lemon meringue pies. Approximately 65 cars are proudly displayed in the Goleta Fall Classic Car, Motorcycle and Hot Rod Show.

PERU: OLMOS

In the middle of June, annually, the festival is held in Olmos on the Eastern edge of the Sechura Desert. Here competitions take place between producers, as well as dances and celebrations being held.

USA: UPLAND

Held in Historic Downtown Upland, the festival offers something for everyone. Children and parents alike, the children have the fun Lemon Zone, including on stage performances, make & take crafts, petting zoo, pony rides and a climbing wall. Whilst adults can indulge in tasting local wines and ice-cold beers at the Beer and Wine Garden. The festival, taking place in April, is also famous for its Western Area where there are live gun shows, famous Western actors and an authentic Native American Teepee. The now famous Lemon Pie Eating Contest is one of the highlights of the community stage.

ITALY: MONTEROSSO

Every year, during May, the village is coloured in yellow. The ancient, narrow streets of the town are the setting for exibitions featuring the lemon and its products such as limoncino, lemon cream, lemon marmalade and lemon pie. The '8000 passi al profumo di limoni' is a walking tour all around Monterosso, departing from the house of Eugenio Montale, Nobel Prize winner for Literature (who has written poems about lemons, the most famous named 'Limoni') and ending in a lemon garden where a farmer explains the utilisation of lemons in many different ways. In the evening music and the awards for the best shop window display are nominated.

MADEIRA

This event was held for the first time in May 2001 at the parish of Ilha in the municipality of Santana. The main purpose was to pay tribute to Santana's agriculture and local farmers but most particularly to one of its main products – the lemon. This festival is characterised by the typical popular religious festivities, including the participation of the local folk dancing groups, brass bands, musicians and other entertainment from the mainland.

FRANCE: MENTON

La Fete Du Citron, is a fabulously zesty citrus festival attended by over 250,000 visitors per year, lasting 3 weeks and taking place annually during February. This pretty seaside place known as La Cité des Citrons; The City of Lemons, is historically intrinsically associated with the utilitarian fruit that is the lemon. Folklore claims Eve, who was chased from paradise to earth, brought this golden fruit with her and because Adam was scared of the wrath of God's anger, he persuaded her to hide it. Eve chose to bury the fruit in Menton, wishing that its rich fertile soil would replicate the paradise she lost. Since then lemons have flourished, later being the inspiration of the town's biggest festival. Part of its uniqueness are the fantastic floats and monumental structures adorned by squillions of lemons and oranges (well, around 140 tons at least). They are displayed night and day in the Biovès gardens. Each year, a different festival theme is chosen; these have included cartoon heroes, the greatest civilisations and the islands of the world. During my four days in the town, apart from attending all of the festivities, time was made to fit in the very important sampling of virtually all local lemon produce available, using the unique essence of the Menton lemon (some would say due to the soil, mountain shade and high essential oil content in its rind). Pailas de Carnoles, hosts the largest citrus collection in Europe, including rare varieties such as the lemon of Sochi (citrus medica). It really is a citrus delight to visit.

USA: CALIFORNIA: CHULA VISTA

Held in the month of August, the festival features a Kids' Fun Zone with non-stop entertainment, including carnival rides, inflatables, rock climbing and community performances. There are also pie eating and largest lemon competitions, as well as an unusual 'Lemon Fantasy Hair Competition' featuring the innovative styles from their Third Avenue salons.

ITALY: SORRENTO

The festival takes place in mid-July, during which local producers and craftsmen exhibit their products. There are antique and photographic exhibitions, as well as folk music performances. Award ceremonies take place for the best olive oil and cheese. The festival is preceded in May by guided walks through the olive, lemon and orange groves, with tourists guided by students of a local foreign language school.

ARGENTINA: TUCUMÁN

Held in the month of June. Every year there is a different twist on their lemon festival, for example, in the past, several students from schools in Tafí Viejo participated in creating the biggest lemonade jar in the world, for which they entered the Guinness World Records. In total, 5·75 litres were produced under the supervision of a public scribe, who around 12:15pm confirmed that the mark of 4·5 litres had been broken and with that, the previous record set by the United States.

DID YOU KNOW?

GOT SECRETS?
WRITE IT WITH A LEMON!

The acid in lemon juice weakens paper, thus when the paper is heated, the remaining acid turns the writing brown before discolouring the paper. The writing turns brown because the weakened paper burns before the rest of the paper. Easy with the heating though, as you don't want to set the paper alight!

Lemon juice

Sunlight or a heat source (such as a light bulb)

Paper

Cotton bud or paintbrush

First get some lemon juice, either from fresh lemons or you could use bottled lemon juice. Pretend that the juice is ink and apply to writing paper with a cotton bud or paintbrush.

Allow the paper to dry. When you are ready to read your invisible message, hold the paper up to sunlight, a light bulb (best), or another heat source. The heat will cause the writing to darken to a pale brown, so your message can now be read.

Alternatively, you could put salt on the drying 'ink'. After 1 minute, wipe the salt off and colour over the paper with a wax crayon to reveal the message.

RUN OUT OF BATTERIES?
USE A LEMON!

This is a popular scientific experiment in schools which involves attaching electrodes to a lemon and using it as a battery to produce electricity. Although not much power is produced, two lemons used together could power a small digital watch.

18 gauge copper wire (smaller gauge will work too, but 18 gauge is stiffer)

Wire clippers

Steel paper clip (some find that a 5cm strip of zinc works better)

Coarse sandpaper

A lemon

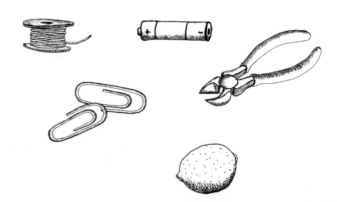

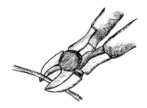

One lemon contains about 15 calories and 0 grams fat.

Lemon was among the first eight flavours of Jelly Belly jelly beans, launched in 1976.

The average lemon contains about 3 tablespoons of juice.

Lemon oil is often used on the unsealed rosewood fingerboards of guitars and other stringed instruments.

The average lemon contains about eight pips.

The citric acid from lemon juice is said to be strong enough to dissolve a pearl.

Surprise: lemons are technically berries (known as hesperdium).

The word lemon is believed to be derived from Asian language words for 'sour' or 'sour fruit'.

It is said the crystal citrine (the name is derived from the colour – the yellow of the lemon) cleanses the emotions and promotes happiness, inner strength and hope. So, carry it with you, to enhance these qualities...

In the 16th century, lemon balm was rubbed on beehives to encourage the bees to make honey.

Remove 5cm of insulation from the copper wire. Slice off the 5cm of bare wire using the clippers. Straighten the paper clip and cut off 5cm of the straightened steel wire, or you could use a 5cm strip of zinc. Use sandpaper to smooth and polish any rough areas on the tips of the wire as well as on the paper clip or strip of zinc.

Roll the lemon under the palm of your hand, on a flat surface, to start the inner juices flowing. Press the paper clip and the wire as close together as possible but without touching, into the lemon.

Now with the tip of your tongue, touch the two free ends of both wires.

You will endure a slight tingling sensation and taste something metallic.

The lemon battery is called a voltaic battery; it changes chemical energy into electrical energy.

A battery consists of two different metals (the steel paper clip and the copper wire). They are called electrodes, the parts of a battery through which the electric current enters and leaves the battery. The electrodes are placed in liquid containing an electrolyte, a solution with the ability to conduct electricity. In a solution of water containing an electrolyte, such as the acid in the lemon, an overabundance of electrons collects at one end of the electrodes. At the same time, electrons are lost from the other electrode.

Touching the electrodes with your tongue closes the circuit, enabling a small electric current to flow. A single lemon can produce 7/10 of a volt of electricity. If you connected two lemons together, you could power a simple digital watch (which uses around 1.5 volts). To do this, take a length of malleable, thin wire to connect the silver wire of one lemon to the copper wire of the other lemon. Then attach thin wires from the other two wires in the lemons to where a battery's positive and negative poles connect and this will power the watch.

If you were wondering... The tingle felt in your tongue along with the metallic flavour is due to the movement of electrons through the saliva on your tongue.

The lemon is an excellent source of vitamin C (a single lemon provides 40–70% of the minimum daily requirement), but it begins to lose its vitamin power soon after it is squeezed. There is a 20% loss of vitamin C after only eight hours at room temperature or 24 hours in the fridge.

Lemons are scientifically known as citrus limon.

For the most antioxidants choose fully ripened lemons.

The major producers of lemons today are Italy, Spain, Greece, United States, Israel and Turkey.

Sour limes possess a greater sugar and citric acid content than lemons and have an acidic, tart taste, while sweet limes lack citric acid content and are sweet in flavour.

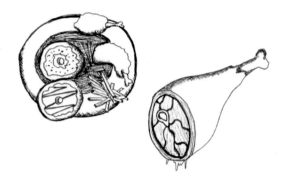

Lemon juice is a powerful antibacterial agent, as has been proved through experiments. The bacteria causing malaria, cholera, diphtheria, typhoid and other deadly diseases can be destroyed by lemon juice.

Lemon juice has a chemical quality that cuts fats and oils. No wonder lemon juice features in dishwashing liquids so often! For the body, it aids fat metabolism, at the same time as helping liver function.

The human tongue can detect a drop of lemon juice diluted in 129,000 drops of water.

Lemons are used to flavour the alcoholic drinks Limoncello in Italy and Limonnaya vodka in Russia.

It has been said the original recipe of eau de cologne consisted of 12 drops each of essential oils of oranges, bergamot, citron neroli and rosemary with a gram of Malabar cardamoms and a gallon of rectified spirits which were all distilled together.

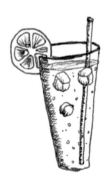

Gin and Tonic with a slice of lemon please... G&T is known to be a refreshing drink but why? Scientists have now discovered it is probably due to the slice of lemon contained within it, this is because they have identified that citrus fruits have a chemical releasing a smell, which reduces stress effects on 109 genes in the human body.

You can never be too thin... thin-skinned lemons are best. Lemons with thicker rinds are less fleshy and likely to be less juicy. Choose lemons that are heavy for their size and have a rind with a finely grained texture. Ideally, they should be bright yellow in colour; those that have green tinges will be more acidic due to the fact that they have not fully ripened. Signs of an overripe fruit include wrinkly skin, soft or hard patches and dull colouring. Luckily fresh lemons are available all year round!

If you see a lemon in a dream, it normally indicates success, happiness and confidence. If you see the juice, however, it

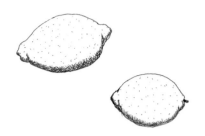

could mean you are bitter. If you drink the juice, it relates to good health. Eating a lemon could be a sign that you will be ill soon, however if you are not eating one, but merely seeing one or many on a tree, this could indicate wealth ahead. Giving someone a lemon implies that you are criticising them. A squeezed lemon could imply exploitation. An old lemon points to divorce or an upcoming split. If you are peeling a lemon, it is showing you that you would escape danger. To see lemons growing on a tree, indicates travel with great experiences. If you see the lemon as a food source, it points to trouble with the authorities. If it is green, it could predict a disease.

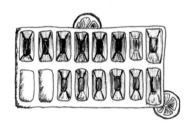

Lemon juice and zest can be stored for later use. Pour freshly squeezed lemon juice into ice cube trays, subsequently storing them in plastic bags, and then freeze them. Dried lemon zest should be stored in a cool, dry place in an airtight glass container.

Essential oil of lemon may have a photosensitising effect on certain people. Therefore wearing a skin product containing it during exposure to the sun could cause a skin reaction. However, this reaction is very uncommon!

Lemons are oval in shape and feature a yellow, texturised outer rind. Like other citrus fruits, the inner flesh is divided into segments, the average lemon has eight to ten.

According to the ancient Hindu science of health and medicine: Ayurveda, a lemon is a valuable fruit, with admirable properties. Lemons are perceived as sour, warm, promoters of gastric fire, light, good for vision, pungent and astringent. Lemon checks the excessive flow of bile and cleanses the mouth. It dislodges phlegm and expels wind from the digestive tract. It aids in digestion and alleviates constipation. It prevents vomiting, throat trouble, acidity and rheumatism. It destroys intestinal worms.

Lemon Verbena   Lemon Grass

Lemons are so good they have impersonators which share some of the same qualities. Among them are lemongrass, lemon balm, lemon thyme, lemon verbena, scented geraniums, certain cultivars of basil, and certain cultivars of mint. Recently the Australian bush food lemon myrtle (p.12) has become a popular alternative to lemons. Limes are often used instead of lemons.

Lemon Mint

Lemon Myrtle

As citrus fruits became more widely available, horticulturalists and cooks attempted many ways of preserving the acid scent of citrus fruit.

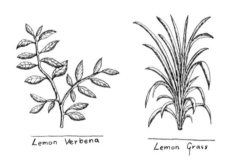

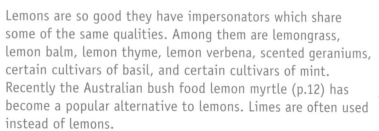

WITHIN
LEMON JUICE there is
13mg of vitamin C per ounce
and 36mg per ounce in the rind.
LEMON EVIL EYE PROTECTOR CHARM
In Sicily a lemon (a liquid-filled, eye-shaped
fruit) is sometimes pierced with nine nails and
placed above a doorway to prevent a jettatore with evil
power from entering. MOST LEMON TREES bear two crops per
year, with the flower and fruit appearing together. The lemons are
usually harvested when green, to be ripened in special storehouses,
those which ripen on the tree have the best flavour but they decay faster
than the ones ripened after being picked. SIMILAR TO MANY MIDDLE EASTERN
COUNTRIES, in Turkey, it is common practice to cup one's hands, fill with a lemon
cologne (limon kolonyası) and wipe over your face, behind your neck or wherever
you like to refresh yourself. It is also offered at religious ceremonies. CITRIC ACID
– lemons were the primary commercial source of this substance before the expansion
of fermentation based processes. A HALVED LEMON is used as a finger moistener for
those counting large amounts of bills such as tellers and cashiers. ICE-SKATING Sculling
is sometimes called 'lemons'. This is when you go forwards and backwards in lemon shapes
on the ice. LEMON JUICE is rich in acid and the pectin it contains makes it ideal for fruits
of poor setting quality such as strawberries, which are being used to make preserves.
LEMON JUICE can be used instead of vinegar to make salad dressings. LEMON ESSENTIAL OIL
can be extracted from a fresh lemon by rubbing lump sugar over the well washed surface
of a lemon. 'THE MARKET FOR LEMONS: QUALITY UNCERTAINTY AND THE MARKET MECHANISM'
is a 1970 paper by the economist George Akerlof. It discusses 'information asymmetry', which
occurs when the seller knows more about a product than the buyer. FRESH LEMONS can be
stored for a few months by wrapping them in greaseproof paper or cellophane. LEMON has
been attested to be a blessing for mountaineers. Edmund Hillary, the first man to put his
foot on the top of Mt. Everest, has admitted that his victory was greatly attributed to
the lemon, due to drinking copious amounts of hot water with lemon to combat the
acute effects of dehydration at altitude. BITE INTO A LEMON to redden your lips
(a common practice in the court of Louis XIV). A FINGER BOWL is a bowl of water, usually
with lemon, which is used for cleansing one's fingers in between courses. LEMON
has been used historically to combat gout and rheumatism. LEMONS have been
used in destroying intestinal worms. THE LEMON is one of nature's top sources
of potassium. LEMONS was a comic strip in the UK comic The Beano. LEMON
LAW is the association of law that offers protection to owners of motor
vehicles with recurrent mechanical or other problems, which are not
solved within an adequate time by the dealer or manufacturer.
THE LEMON TRICK made famous by Emil Jarrow, involved him
borrowing a banknote, proceeding to make it disappear.
He would then offer a lemon to be examined, cut it
in two and reveal the missing, crisp paper
money within it. The trick's illusion
depended on him piercing
the lemon using his
particularly strong
thumb.

A LEMON IS A **DEFECTIVE CAR** that is found to have many or severe flaws not noted before its purchase. Any vehicle with these issues can be termed a 'lemon' and, by extension, any product which has major defects that prove it unfit for its purpose can be described as a 'lemon'. Good used cars however, are called cherries. **LEMON SOCIALISM** is a disparaging term for government support of private-sector companies whose imminent collapse is alleged to threaten broader economic stability. It is not a current within socialism, rather, it suggests a bribery of free-market capitalist systems, which would normally allow defective companies 'lemons' to fail. **THE LEMON TECHNIQUE** is a process used by meteorologists utilising weather radar to determine the relative strength of thunderstorm cells in a vertically sheared environment. **THE LEMON GROVE INCIDENT** was an occasion that happened in 1930 and 1931 in Lemon Grove, California, where the local school board endeavoured to build a separate school for children of Mexican origin. **THE 24 HOURS OF LEMONS** is a series of endurance races taking place on paved road race courses across the United States. The title is a parody of the historic 24 Hours of Le Mans series. Teams compete in races using cars that cost no more than $500 ie 'lemons' for up to 24 hours. These races stand out from the usual road race owing to its odd penalties and punishments. **THE LEMON SLICE NEBULA**, or IC 3568, is a planetary nebula in the constellation Camelopardalis. **THE LEMON SQUEEZER** is a noteworthy rock formation in Harriman State Park, New York. **THE MASTER CLEANSE**, also known as the Lemon Cleanse and the Maple Syrup Diet, is a liquid diet created by Stanley Burroughs in 1941. The Master Cleanse claims to be a method to cleanse the body of, and remove the cravings associated with drugs, alcohol, tobacco, eating, coffee and tea. The cleanse involves drinking only a concoction made from fresh lemons, grade B maple syrup and cayenne pepper, as well as a laxative tea. No solid food is eaten for the entire cleanse. **A LEFT-HANDED LEMON** could be called an 'orange'. Lemons and oranges have the exact same chemical structure, but the opposite way around, so it is a mirror-image. Therefore, the smell of an orange is precisely opposite to that of a lemon. **IN JAPAN** the essential oil of lemon is diffused through the air systems of offices and factories as it increases concentration and the ability to memorise, significantly reducing mistakes. Research has confirmed that the aroma of lemon is relaxing to brain waves, which improves concentration. It was the most effective essential oil tested in reducing computer errors; those working in a lemon scented room made less than half the mistakes of those working in unscented rooms. Because it appears to stimulate the mind whilst calming emotions, therefore sniffing lemon can be helpful when making decisions. **SEA SILK** is a tremendously fine, rare and expensive fabric created from the long silky filaments secreted by a gland in the foot of numerous bivalve molluscs. They manage to do this by attaching themselves to the sea bed. When it is treated with lemon juice, it turns into a stunning golden colour which will never fade.

LEMON HISTORY

Like many other fruits and vegetables, lemons were brought to the Americas by Christopher Columbus on his second voyage to the New World in 1493. They have been grown in Florida since the 16th century, when they began to be used in cooking and for flavouring.

It is thought their first journey to Europe was initiated by Arabs who brought them to Spain in the 11th century around the same time that they were introduced to North Africa.

The Crusaders, who found the fruit growing in Palestine, have been credited with bringing the lemon to other countries across Europe.

Lemons, like other vitamin C rich fruits, were highly prized by prospectors and miners during the California Gold Rush in the mid-19th century, to protect them against scurvy.

It is said lemons were originally developed as a cross between the lime and the citron. They are thought to have originated in China, North Burma or India, having been cultivated in these regions for about 2,500 years. They were later exported to Persia and then to Iraq and Egypt circa 700 AD.

Lemons were in such demand that people were willing to pay up to $1 per fruit, a price that would still be deemed costly today and was very expensive in 1849.

Lemons were historically considered sacred in Muslim countries, where they were used as an astringent against dysenteric and haemorrhagic symptoms, as well as to keep the Devil away from homes.

Lemons as an ornamental plant were a highlight in early Islamic gardens.

Traditionally in South and Southeast Asia and Mesopotamian civilisations, lemons were known for their antiseptic properties and were exploited as an antidote for various poisons. They also have anti-rheumatic and refreshing properties.

In ancient times women used to use lemon douches as a recommended form of contraception.

Ancient Egyptians used lemons to embalm their mummies, frequently putting them in tombs with dates and figs.

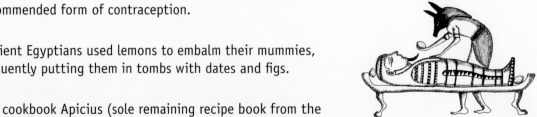

The cookbook Apicius (sole remaining recipe book from the days of the Roman Empire) mentions the Citrus Medica.

It is rumoured that the first real lemon cultivation in Europe began in Genoa in the middle of the 15th century.

According to some sources, the Spanish conquest throughout the New World helped spread lemon seeds.

A citron is similar to a lemon, but it is larger, with a very thick rind and little pulp and juice. It is said to have been documented by the ancient Jews before the time of Christ.

Although there are depictions of citrus fruits from Roman mosaics in Carthage and frescoes in Pompeii that bear a strong resemblance to oranges and lemons, apparently this iconographical evidence is not supported by any paleobotanical or literary verification, suggesting therefore the artists either imported the fruits or saw them in the East.

Apparently Sicilians took some centuries to understand what a blessing lemons were for them, as Sicily was not always the country of lemons. Intensive farming of lemons and citrus fruits on the island only started in the 17th century by the Jesuits.

Pliny, the Roman author, naturalist and philosopher, spoke about the lemon in his treatments, prescribing it as an antidote against various toxins.

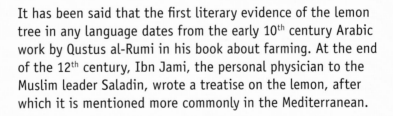

It has been said that the first literary evidence of the lemon tree in any language dates from the early 10th century Arabic work by Qustus al-Rumi in his book about farming. At the end of the 12th century, Ibn Jami, the personal physician to the Muslim leader Saladin, wrote a treatise on the lemon, after which it is mentioned more commonly in the Mediterranean.

It has been suggested that Greeks imported lemons from Media and used them as decoration as well as to freshen linen, protecting it from moths. They used a bed of lemon leaves as a pillow under the head of the dead. The first clear descriptions of the usage of lemon for therapeutic purposes date back to the works of Theophrastus, Aristotle's pupil, who is thought to be the founder of phytotherapy.

Hellenics used to grow lemon trees near olive trees to preserve them from parasitic attacks.

In the early part of the 20th century, Lemon was a common first name. There were thousands of American boys and girls named Lemon in the 1900 census.

It has been said in 1494 lemons appeared in the Azores.

Egyptians of the 14th century were aware of lemons. Along the Egyptian Mediterranean coast, people drank kashkab, a drink made of fermented barley and mint, rue, black pepper, and citron leaf. It has been mooted that lemonade may have had its origin in medieval Egypt. Although the lemon originates further to the East and it is probable lemonade was invented in one of the Eastern countries; the earliest written evidence of lemonade comes from Egypt. The first reference to the lemon in Egypt is in the chronicles of the Persian poet and traveller Nasir-i-Khusraw, who left a useful account of life in Egypt under the Fatamid caliph al-Mustansir. Trade in lemon juice was vast by 1104. Documents found in the Cairo Geniza, the records of the medieval Jewish community in Cairo from the 10th–12th centuries, state that bottles of lemon juice called Qatarmizat were made with substantial amounts of sugar and were consumed locally as well as exported.

The Roman Emperor Nero, is said to have been very fond of lemons, with insinuations it was due to his obsession with the premonition that he might be poisoned.

In 1747, James Lind's experiments on seamen suffering from scurvy (a disease widespread among sailors who lived for long periods chiefly eating flours and preserved food), ascertained that scurvy was a result of a serious and prolonged deficiency of vitamin C (ascorbic acid) within their diet. Therefore lemons were widely stocked on ships to consume, ultimately combating the disease successfully.

Cloves and lemons have been partners for a long while. A knight from the French crusades, would woo a lady by gifting her with a clove pierced lemon, both were expensive at that time, ergo an impressive gesture. The 20th century embraces the Cloved Lemon Kissing Game, whereby particular groups use a clove pierced lemon in order to kiss a desired one.

It has been said the name 'lemon' originated from the Arabic līmūn ليمون and Persian limun via old Italian and old French limone.

EASY PEASY LEMON SQUEEZY PRESERVED LEMONS

Extremely simple to make...

20	**unwaxed lemons, cut lengthwise into quarters**
6 tsp	**salt**
2 tsp	**paprika**
4 tbsp	**coriander seeds**
	Olive oil, to cover
2–4	**cinnamon sticks***

Begin by putting the lemon quarters into a colander, sprinkle with the salt and leave to rest overnight. Now arrange the quarters in your sterilised jars alternating with a sprinkling of paprika and seeds. Completely cover with olive oil, add cinnamon sticks, 1 per jar, seal tightly and leave for 4 weeks in the fridge before using in dishes like Mint Chicken with Caramelised Onions & Almonds (p.220).

*depending on how many jars you use to store the lemons – 1 stick per jar

LEMONS IN LIFE

SEA LEMON

is a common name for a group of invertebrate colourful sea slugs or Nudibranchs.

LEMON TETRA

(Hyphessobrycon Pulchripinnis) is a popular aquarium fish, originating from South America.

LEMON SHARK

(Negaprion Brevirostris) is a shark belonging to the family Carcharhinidae, growing up to 3m long. It is so-called for the 'citrus glands' under its skin that exude a lemony scent to attract prey.

SICKLEFIN LEMON SHARK

or Sharp Tooth Lemon Shark (Negaprion Acutidens) is a species of Requiem Shark (family of Carcharhinidae) found within the tropical waters of the Indo-Pacific. It is closely related to the prevalent Lemon Shark (Negaprion Brevirostris) of the Americas; the two species are almost identical in shape, large bodied sharks with wide heads, two dorsal fins, and a plain yellow tinged blush.

LEMON MYRTLE

(Backhousia Citriodora, Lemon Scented Myrtle, Lemon scented Ironwood) is a flowering plant in the family Myrtaceae, genus Backhousia. An Australian native tree with a noticeable lemon aroma, used in cooking and as an anti-bacterial agent. For a tasty drink recipe, go to p.90.

AFRICAN LEMON DOVE

or Cinnamon Dove (Columba Larvata) is a bird species in the pigeon family (Columbidae).

TOXOPTERA CITRICIDA

is a species of aphid also known as the Brown Citrus Aphid, Black Citrus Aphid, and Oriental Citrus Aphid. It was first discovered in Florida in 1995. It is a feared pest of citrus because it is a vector for the pathogenic plant virus Citrus Tristeza. The aphid distributed the virus throughout many citrus groves in Brazil and Venezuela during the 1970s, contributing to the virtual destruction of their citrus industry.

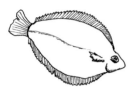

SOUTHERN LEMON SOLE

(Pelotretis Flavilatus) is a Righteye Flounder, the only species in the genus Pelotretis, seen throughout New Zealand in enclosed waters such as estuaries, harbours, mudflats, and sandflats, in waters less than 385m in depth. They measure 25–50cm in length.

LEMON-BREASTED SEEDEATER

(Serinus Citrinipectus), also known as the Lemon-Breasted Canary, is a species of finch in the Fringillidae family.

LEMON-BELLIED CROMBEC

(Sylvietta Denti) is a species of African Warbler, formerly placed in the family Sylviidae.

LEMON-BREASTED BERRYPECKER

is a species of bird in the Melanocharitidae family.

LEMON MINT

(Monarda Citriodora), also known as Purple Horse Mint or Lemon Beebalm, is a member of the mint family (Lamiaceae), which has a citrus aroma when pressed, akin to the fruit of the lemon plant, its purple flowers are attractive to bees and hummingbirds.

LEMON GLOW

(Banksia) a form of Banksia Spinulosa var. Cunninghamii with lemon yellow flowers.

LEMON-CHESTED GREENLET

(Hylophilus Thoracicus) is a species of bird of the Vireonidae family found in South America.

LEMON-BELLIED FLYROBIN

(Microeca Flavigaster) is a species of bird belonging to the Petroicidae family.

LEMONGRASS

(Cymbopogon) is a genus of around 55 species of grasses, native to warm temperate and tropical areas of the Old World and Oceania. It is a tall perennial grass.

LEMON BASIL

(Ocimum x Citriodorum) is a hybrid between basil (Ocimum Basilicum) and African Basil (Ocimum Americanum). The herb is grown primarily in North Eastern Africa and Southern Asia for its sharp lemon scent when used in cooking. In Laos, Lemon Basil is particularly used in curries, stews, and stir-fried dishes. Lemon Basil is also popular in the cuisine of Indonesia, where is it called 'kemangi' often eaten raw as lalab (raw fresh vegetables) and used as a seasoning for soups and salads, or as a garnish. It is also a main ingredient in pepes (marinated steamed meat).

LEMON ANT

(Myrmelachista schumanni) is a species of ant that is important for the formation of 'Devil's Gardens'. Utilising its own herbicide, it is capable of moulding its surroundings.

LEMON-THROATED BARBET

(Eubucco Richardsoni) is a species of bird belonging to the Capitonidae family. It is found in the Western Amazon basin.

LEMON DAY-LILY,

Lemon Lily or Yellow Daylily (Hemerocallis Flava) is a plant of the genus Hemerocallis.

LEMON-BROWED FLYCATCHER

(Conopias Cinchoneti) is a species of bird belonging to the Tyrannidae family.

LEMON PANSY

(Junonia Lemonias) is a Nymphalid butterfly commonly found in South Asia.

LEMON PLEUROBRANCH

(Berthellina granulata) is a species of sea slug.

LEMON BOTTLEBRUSH

also known as Crimson Bottlebrush, Callistemon citrinus, is an Australian native evergreen shrub, which thrives in bright sun, warm temperatures and dry air. It doesn't actually have petals, each "bottle brush" flower is made up of bright red stamens with yellow tips, clustered on flower spikes up to 10cm long. They have a fragrant, lemony scent, hence the name Lemon Bottlebrush.

LEMON SOLE
(Microstomus Kitt) is a flatfish of the family Pleuronectidae. It lives in the shallow waters of Northern Europe, but it is not a sole, it is actually a flounder!

LEMON-SPECTACLED TANAGER
(Chlorothraupis Olivacea) is a species of bird in the Cardinalidae family.

LEMON-BELLIED WHITE-EYE
(Zosterops Chloris) is a species of bird living in Indonesia.

LEMON ASPEN
(Acronychia Acidula) is a rainforest tree found in Queensland, Australia.

LEMON YELLOW ROSEMALLOW
(Hibiscus calyphyllus, syn. Hibiscus calycinus, Hibiscus chrysantha, Hibiscus chrysanthus, Hibiscus rockii) is a Hibiscus shrub from tropical Africa. It grows up to 1–1·8m tall and has flowers with a diameter of 8–10cm that are bright yellow with a brownish centre.

LEMON BUD MOTH
(Prays Parilis) is a moth of the Yponomeutidae family.

LEMON DROP MANGOSTEEN
is the name used for two species of tropical American fruit trees.

LEMON DOTTED BORDER
(Mylothris sagala), the Dusky Dotted, is a butterfly in the Pieridae family. It is found in Ethiopia, Kenya, Tanzania, the Democratic Republic of Congo, Rwanda, Malawi, Zambia and Zimbabwe. It lives in sub-montane and montane forests.

LEMON BALM
(Melissa Officinalis) is a perennial herb in the mint family Lamiaceae, native to Southern Europe and the Mediterranean region.

LEMON TITBITS

LEMON TITBITS

The random usefulness of lemons...

BLENDING
Add a couple of lemon drops to a blender to prevent your veg or fruit going brown.

SALAD DRESSING
Combine lemon juice with olive or flax oil, freshly crushed garlic and pepper to make a light and refreshing salad dressing – yum scrum.

VITAMIN C
To retain as much vitamin C as possible, add lemon juice at the end of a cooked recipe.

FLUFFY RICE
Add some lemon juice when cooking rice to make it fluffier and whiter, as well as preventing the rice from sticking to the sides, making cleaning a lot easier.

CRISPY DUCK
To make chicken or duck skin extra crispy, rub with lemon juice before cooking, healthier than salt.

CLEAN?
Unless the establishment looks super-duper clean, rethink accepting lemon slices in your drinks, due to their preparation perhaps not being ultra hygienic.

FIGHT BACTERIA
Add lemon juice to 'dodgy' drinking water to help combat bacteria.

LEMON TWISTS
Strips (twists) of lemon peel are attractive in cocktails, sparkling water, and tap water. Use a knife or vegetable peeler to produce long strips, cutting away the bitter white pith. It is possible to make them in advance, and then freeze, in a freezer friendly container or bag until needed.

NO NEED TO THROW OUT LIMP LETTUCE
Put in a bowl of cold water with a tablespoon of lemon juice and leave it for half an hour. Remove and shake dry.

LEMON EXTRACT POWDER
Having produced lemon zest or twists, ensuring the pith is removed, dry the strips skin-side down on a plate until they are completely dehydrated, around three or four days. Put in a blender (or spice grinder) and pulverise into a powder. Use the powdered peel in place of extract or zest in recipes.

"When life gives you lemons, you make lemonade. I have several stands around here"
– James Brady

LEMON SUGAR

Having made lemon extract powder (opposite page) simply add to sugar. Alternatively, you can use fresh twists, placing them in a jar with sugar to allow the peels oil to infuse the sugar. Similar to Russian Lemon Sugar (p.234).

LEMON PEPPER

Mix lemon extract powder (opposite page) with freshly cracked pepper. Ideal with meats (particularly chicken) pasta, and most definitely fish. It may also be used to season tofu.

LEMON ZEST

Lemon zest is simply grated lemon peel and is the quintessence of lemon essence. It can be used fresh, dried, or frozen. If you don't have a zester, you can use the smallest size of a box grater (note: it is much easier to grate the zest from the lemon before juicing them). To dry zest, spread it on a kitchen towel and leave it out until dehydrated, then store in a jar. To freeze, use a freezer safe container. Use zest in salads, marinades, baked goods... The possibilities are endless...

BITTER LEMON

One of my favourite soft drinks, a carbonated drink flavoured with quinine and lemon, the bitterness derives from lemon pith, lemon rind and of course quinine, its lemon zing is the main differentiation from tonic water.

FISH

Place thinly sliced lemons underneath and around fish before baking or grilling, it will soften the slices so that they can be eaten along with the fish. When fish is grilled on top of lemon slices, it will prevent the fish from sticking to the grill.

KEEP BROWN SUGAR SOFT

If your brown sugar hardens into a brick, try adding some lemon peel (all traces of pulp and pith removed) to help keep it moist and easy to use.

EGGS

Prevent eggs from cracking when boiling by coating the shells with lemon juice. Ensure easy peeling of cooked eggs by adding one teaspoon of lemon juice to the cooking water!

AVOCADOS, APPLES, BANANAS...

When lemon juice is sprinkled on certain foods that tend to oxidise and turn brown after being sliced, such as apples, bananas and avocados, the acid acts as a short term preservative by denaturing the enzymes that cause browning and deterioration.

GREMOLATA

Is a mixture of lemon zest, finely chopped garlic and parsley, a yummy and healthy alternative to salt and pepper.

SALT SUBSTITUTE

Serve lemon wedges with meals as their tartness makes a great salt substitute.

"At my lemonade stand I used to give the first glass away free and charge five dollars for the second glass. The refill contained the antidote"
– Emo Philips

DRY CAKE

Drizzle over some freshly squeezed lemon juice.

VINEGAR

Lemon juice can easily be substituted for vinegar.

CREAM

Add as much lemon juice as it takes to single cream to make it into thick, whipping cream.

C C LEMON

Is a Japanese soft drink invented by Suntory. Known for both its lemon flavour and adverts featuring characters from *The Simpsons*.

LEMON & PAEROA (L&P)

Is a saccharine-sweetened soft drink manufactured in New Zealand. Originally made by combining lemon juice and carbonated mineral water from the town of Paeroa, now manufactured by multi-national Coca Cola.

LEMON DROPS

Sugary, lemon flavoured sweets, typically coloured yellow and shaped like a miniature lemon.

KEEP IT WHITE

Add lemon juice to rice, cauliflower, or potatoes while cooking to enhance their white colour.

LEMON MYRTLE LEAF

Add a roughly shredded lemon Myrtle leaf to cooked rice to accompany a curry.

PAPAYA

Squeeze lemon juice onto a papaya half and eat it at its best.

BAKED GOODS

Include dried lemon peel for yummy flavouring.

THE LEMON DROP

Is a fiery, citrus flavoured pepper, a popular seasoning pepper in Peru, where it is known as Kellu Uchu.

CITRUS PLANT POT

You can use your leftover lemon halves as a mini plant pot to start off most seedlings. First, remove all of the pulp, fill with soil, choose your seedling – any plant that you would normally start indoors would work planted in a citrus half. Now watch it grow! When the seedling is around 5cm in height, plant it (citrus peel and all) in the garden.

GARNISH

To make the most of lemon as a garnish on a drink, rub the outside of the rind of the lemon on the edge of the glass. The result is a hint of lemon with each sip.

"I believe that if life gives you lemons, you should make lemonade... And try to find somebody whose life has given them vodka, and have a party"
– Ron White

SIERRA MIST

Is a lemon/lime flavoured caffeine-free soft drink, launched by PepsiCo in 2000.

LEMON JELLO

Is a type of food, similar to lemon curd, but made from jelly, instead of curd.

SHERBET LEMONS

These popular sweets in the UK are lemon-flavoured, hard-boiled candies encasing a fizzy sherbet centre – love them!

LEMON JUICE TO MARINATE MEAT

The acid provided by the juice partially hydrolises the tough collagen fibres in the meat, thus tenderising it.

DRIED LEMON SLICES

These make a terrific garnish. Just cut unpeeled fruit into 2mm thick slices, discarding the ends. Place on a large wire rack on a baking sheet and dry in an 80°C (170°F) oven for 4 hours. Remove from the oven to air-dry.

SUNDAY ROAST

Pierce a whole lemon a number of times with a fork, then stuff it in the cavity of a chicken or turkey before roasting. This will keep the breast meat moist and imbue the whole bird with a luscious flavour.

SUMMER LEMONS

Freeze lemon juice in ice cube trays to use in summer drinks. You could also try grating fine lemon zest into your ice cube trays before freezing, drop a few lemon infused cubes into any cool drink for a pretty and quirky twist.

LEMON SOUR

A soda often used in cocktails.

ENHANCE

When added with fruits and vegetables lemons can vastly enhance their flavour.

AIR FRESHENER

Cut the lemon in half and remove the pulp, fill the empty shell with some salt, and place it at the back of your fridge to keep it lemony fresh. To prevent it tipping over, place on a small dish, you could also tuck one behind the toilet in the bathroom. The salt absorbs the stale and nasty odours, releasing a lemon fragrance.

GROW YOUR OWN LEMON TREE

Simply dry pips with a paper towel. Put in a fridge for a few days enabling them to cool, which encourages them to germinate. In a plant pot cover pips with multi-purpose compost. Place pot in a sunny place if possible and water regularly. Note that lemon trees have thorns, so try and ensure no-one pricks themselves on it.

*Wash: "Gotta ave a quick Lemon Squash" Word: "ave a Lemon Curd with yourself"
– Cockney rhyming slang*

LEMON LIFESTYLE HINTS

WHEN LIFE GIVES YOU LEMONS, CLEAN YOUR HOUSE WITH THEM!

Here are some handy tips to follow.

LEMON AND SALT TO BRIGHTEN COPPER, BRASS, CHROME OR STAINLESS STEEL

If your brass or copper utensils, or kitchen sink, have lost their shine, cut a fresh lemon in half, sprinkle some salt (you can also use baking soda, fire ashes or cream of tartar) onto the surface and rub with the cut side of the lemon. A sparkle will appear almost immediately. The acid in the lemon strips away the build-up of grime whilst the coarse salt scrubs the dirt away. Rinse the utensil under the tap and buff dry with a soft cotton cloth.

CLEAN LEMON JUICE STAINS OFF MARBLE

Make a paste by mixing baking soda with water. Apply it onto the stained surface, after it is dry, wipe it off with a damp soft cloth. Lastly dry it with another soft cloth or towel. Note, always be careful when cutting lemons near marble, as it can be sensitive to the acid.

MUM SAYS

Put lemon rind on the radiator, cut into nice shapes, as it dries, the room will be filled with a pleasant citrus smell. The dried pieces can be used in flower displays, or added decoration at Christmas time...

Keep insects away from stored clothing using dried lemon rind dotted in amongst your wardrobe.

LEMON IN THE HOUSE...

The juice is roughly 5–6% citric acid with a pH level of around 2–3. This low pH acidity makes lemon juice indispensible in breaking down rust and mineral stains, yet gentle enough not to dull finishes. There is normally sufficient juice in used lemon halves to tackle small tasks, and it all comes with its own applicator, the rind! On top of this, the oil in the rind is perfect to clean most culinary utensils.

Fill bowls or vases with whole lemons to create elegant table centrepieces.

Dry slices of lemon to use in holiday decorations such as wreaths or garlands, or to include in pot pourri mixtures.

Rid your hands of stains from berries, beetroots, or ink with lemon and salt. Remove a stain from white linens. Just rub the affected area with a cut edge of lemon, then hang to dry in bright sunlight.

Remove garlic, onion, or fish odour from your hands by rubbing them with a piece of lemon coated in salt.

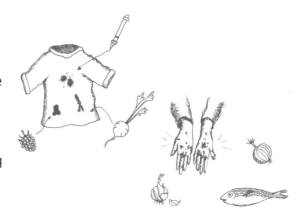

CLEAN YOUR KETTLE OR COFFEE POT THE NATURAL WAY

If you have a mineral deposit build-up in your kettle, fill it with water, adding a handful of thin slices of lemon peel and bring to the boil. Turn off heat and let sit for an hour, drain, and rinse well. For coffee pots, add ice, salt and lemon rinds to the empty pot, shake for a minute or two, discard and rinse.

CLEAN YOUR MICROWAVE

Ditch harsh chemical cleaners and pop lemon rinds into a microwave safe bowl filled halfway with water. Cook on high for 5 minutes, allowing the water to boil and the steam clean the inside. After 5 minutes, take out the bowl and wipe away the grime.

NATURAL CITRUS OVEN CLEANER

Use equal amounts of lemon juice and salt. Apply as a paste to stubborn stains and allow to sit for 3–5 minutes. Scrub with a brush and wipe clean.

DEODORISE YOUR KITCHEN AND MAKE IT SMELL ZESTY!

To wash and deodorise the fridge, waste bins or kitchen compost container, use a solution of 1 teaspoon lemon juice to 1 litre water.

KEEP INSECTS OUT

Many pests abhor the acid in lemon. Leave lemon peel along thresholds, windowsills, and near any cracks or holes where ants or pests may be entering. Adding lemon juice to your floor cleaner helps the repelling of insects.

MAKE A SCENTED HUMIDIFIER

Put lemon peels in a saucepan of water and simmer on the lowest heat to humidify as well as scent the air.

REFRESH CUTTING BOARDS

Due to a lemon's low pH level, it has antibacterial properties that make it a great choice for refreshing cutting boards. After proper disinfecting give the surface a rub with a halved lemon, let sit for a few minutes, and rinse.

DISINFECT AND REFRESH KITCHEN SPONGES

Soak them in water, spiked with lemon juice, put in the microwave on high for 1 minute.

TOILET DOES NOT FLUSH PROPERLY?

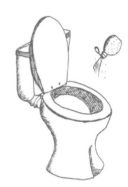

This could be a build-up of lime scale. Take the top off the cistern and pour a small bottle of lemon juice into it, leave for 3 hours, then the toilet should be fine.

Remove stubborn rust stains from the toilet bowl: make a paste of household borax and lemon juice and apply to the stain with a scrubbing brush, let it sit for up to 2 hours, then wipe away.

COUNT ALL THOSE NOTES

Use a halved lemon as a finger moistener for counting large amounts of notes.

NATURAL BLEACH

Chlorine in bleach can be harsh on your clothes, the environment and your wallet, so replace with something better – a lemon – to whiten clothes. Add the juice of 8 lemons to the wash cycle to enhance the whitening action of your laundry detergent.

REMOVE MOST STAINS FROM CLOTHING

Pour lemon juice over the stain, rub the area with salt and place the garment out in the sun for several hours. Wash as usual.

SANITISE

Rub half a lemon over the surface that needs to be sanitised, rinse with water. Use a paste of lemon juice and baking soda to remove stains from plastic storage containers.

GET RID OF UNWANTED ANTS

Trace the ant column back to their point of entry and sprinkle lemon juice, which can also be soaked into a piece of string.

MAKE FLEAS FLEE FOR GOOD!

Citrus is a natural flea deterrent. Pour 240ml boiling water over a chopped up lemon in a bowl, leave to soak overnight and sponge on your dog to kill fleas instantly.

BYE BYE MOSQUITOES...

Lemongrass (Cymbopogon citratus) is a natural and effective mosquito repellent. It contains citronella, a natural oil, that is safe and effective. In fact, the citronella from lemongrass is considered by some to be more effective than true citronella as an insect repellent. You can crush a lemongrass stem and dip it in hot water to rub on your skin.

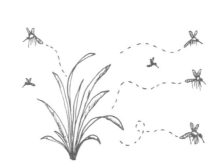

SKIN SOLUTION FOR PETS WITH MANGE

Thinly slice a whole lemon, including the rind. Add it to 1 pint of near-boiling water and let it steep overnight. The next day, sponge the solution onto the animal's skin and let it dry.

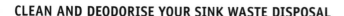

CLEAN AND DEODORISE YOUR SINK WASTE DISPOSAL

Put the peel down the drain, and run the disposal for several minutes. The limonene, which is a naturally occurring chemical in the peel, will dissolve a build-up of food. It also kills odour and leaves your kitchen smelling fresh.

MAKE MOTHS MOVE ON FOR GOOD...

Dried lemon peels are a natural moth deterrent, just toss into your wardrobe, or tie in cheesecloth and hang in the closet.

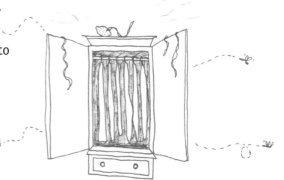

GLASS CARE

Make hard water stains, debris and other marks on glass disappear: Use lemon juice on a sponge or dilute a few tablespoons in a cup of water and spray it on. Wipe it off with newspaper for a totally transparent finish.

FURNITURE POLISH, THE NATURAL WAY

Chemical and fragrance-free, so does not irritate allergies,
plus environmentally friendly.

RECIPE 1

White vinegar
Lemon juice

Mix equal parts of white vinegar and lemon juice,
and decant into a spray bottle. Spray sparingly onto
furniture and polish with a clean cloth. Using another
clean cloth, wipe dry.

RECIPE 2

240ml **olive oil**
120ml **lemon juice**

Use same method as above.

Notes:
Always use a clean spray bottle for both recipes.
Before using, shake well.
Using the same ratios as given, it is possible to make
smaller batches.

LEMON TIPS

JUICING LEMONS

You can either use a reamer, juicer or indeed squeeze by hand. Lemons significantly produce more juice when warm, so best to keep them at room temperature. Rolling them under the palm of your hand on a table will help to extract more juice. Instead of removing any visible seeds before juicing the halves, wait until after the process is complete, as seeds normally sit deep inside the fruit and therefore are not visible on the surface, this will save you a lot of time digging for them.

CUTTING LEMONS

First wash the skin so that any dirt or bacteria residing on the surface will not be transferred inside the fruit.

OBTAINING THE ZEST

Use lemons which are organic and unwaxed, as most conventionally grown lemons contain pesticides. After washing and drying the lemon, use a zester, fine grater, paring knife or vegetable peeler to remove the zest. Careful not to include the white bitter pith directly under the zest.

LEMON WAX COATINGS

Conventionally grown lemons might be waxed to protect them from bruising during shipping. Plant, insect, animal or petroleum-based waxes are often used. Carnauba palm is the most common plant source wax. Other compounds, such as ethyl alcohol or ethanol, are added to the waxes for consistency, milk casein (a protein linked to milk allergy) for 'film formers' and soaps for flowing agents. Since you may not be able to determine the source of these waxes, this is another good reason to choose unwaxed organically grown lemons.

STORING LEMONS

Lemons will stay fresh kept at room temperature, away from exposure to sunlight, for roughly a week. To store for longer, you could keep the lemons in the fridge where they will keep for about a month. Zest can also be stored for later use. Dried lemon zest is best stored in a cool, dry place in an airtight glass container.

BEST WAY TO CUT A LEMON WEDGE

Remove any stickers, rinse the lemon under water and dry. Cut off both ends of the lemon, just enough so that the lemon wedges will have clean edges. Stand the lemon upright, to prevent it from wobbling and cut the lemon from top to bottom. Now cut the 2 halves into as many wedges as desired. To produce a clean finish, slice off the inner edge of the segment, after removing any visible seeds.

LEMON-AID
HEALTH & BEAUTY

LEMON-AID! HEALTH & BEAUTY

Medical precautions: if you suffer from chronic heartburn, kidney or gall-bladder problems or have a citrus allergy, consult your doctor before using these remedies or drinking lemon juice. Some advise that rubbing the skin with lemon juice or oil and drinking lemon juice is not suitable for children under the age of ten. Lemons are definitely effective home remedies for a variety of health concerns but in the case of serious illness always consult your doctor first.

Lemons are highly beneficial and are a natural way to enhance your inner beauty, not to mention the fact that if you follow these awesome lemon beauty tips, you could also dramatically save money. Need any more excuses?

Because lemons are loaded with fruit acids they are able to gently remove dead skin cells and bleach darkened or discoloured areas. Lemon is a natural bleach because it reduces the melanin without any chance of the sort of chemical allergic reaction you could experience with hair dyes and bleaches. It is more beneficial to use freshly squeezed juice, as opposed to bottled, which contains anti-oxidising chemicals which can be harmful to the skin. As well as organically rich in fruit acids, lemon juice also contains natural sugars.

Lemons contain a high amount of vitamin C, with its juice being a natural antioxidant, deactivating free radicals and containing qualities that help stimulate collagen production in the skin. Lemons contain unique flavonoid compounds that have anti-cancer properties. Lemon has been reported as an anti-carcinogenic that lowers the rate of colon, prostate and breast cancer. It prevents metabolism malfunctions in cells, which can predispose a cell to becoming carcinogenic and also blocks the formation of nitrosamines in the gut. Due to the digestive attributes of lemon juice, symptoms of indigestion such as heartburn, bloating and belching are relieved. By drinking lemon juice regularly, you are helping the bowels to eliminate waste more efficiently, therefore controlling constipation and diarrhoea. If you are consuming a lot of lemon juice as laid out in the following tips, protect your tooth enamel by drinking it through a straw.

BOOST YOUR NUTRITION

Eat more alkaline as part of your lifestyle. The virtues of alkaline eating were introduced by Dr Robert Young. He points out that the body is alkaline by nature but all of its functions produce acid. Therefore the body's need for alkaline is constant and what we eat and drink helps buffer the acids that we produce. It has been said that Young even puts alkaline tablets in his coffee to neutralise its acidity. Put simply, alkaline is about the relationship between the food we put in our mouths and our health, as opposed to a fad diet all about weight and outward appearance. To help increase your alkaline intake drink lemon juice in warm water every morning. Lemon although acidic in taste, is alkaline once it is broken down in the digestive system. It has been advocated that alkaline foods should make up to 70% of your diet. Lemon is also a good alkaline substitute for acidic vinegar.

DUMP DEPRESSION WITH A LEMON!

Lemon balm (Melissa officinalis) is actually a type of mint. Its leaves have traditionally been used as a herbal remedy for depression and anxiety, it is also supposed to improve memory storage and recall. Dried leaves are available at health food shops and can be made into a tea, garnished with a slice of lemon. Alternatively use freshly squeezed lemon juice. Listen to joyful music and sip a fresh lemonade, it is uplifting for body and soul.

HAND CREAM

Make your own by mixing 2 parts of glycerine with 1 part of lemon juice.

SORE THROAT

Dilute equal measures of lemon juice with water and gargle often. If you can, it is even better to gargle with pure lemon juice. Alternatively gargling with lemon essential oil (2 drops diluted in ½ glass water) is also helpful.

EMPHYSEMIA

Drink 1 teaspoon of fresh lemon juice 5 times a day. Due to the lemon acidity and high vitamin C content, symptoms should subside.

GET RID OF OILY SKIN

Whip up the white of an egg with a few drops of lemon juice. Apply and leave for 15 minutes before washing off.

CORNS

Bind with a slice of lemon overnight, which will greatly relieve the pain.

FELON: PUS FORMATION ON A FINGER JOINT

A slice of lemon bound over it will draw the pus to the surface where it can easily be removed.

NATURAL HIGHLIGHTS

For sun-kissed hair, on a sunny day, drip lemon juice onto your wet hair, then sit in the sun leaving hair to dry naturally.

ASTHMA

Swallow a tablespoon of lemon juice 1 hour before each meal.

FRESHEN UP IN THE SUMMER HEAT

Rub the inside of some lemon peel across your face for an instant zing.

LIVER COMPLAINTS

First thing when you wake, preferably one hour before breakfast every morning, drink fresh lemon juice in warm water. This helps clear the digestive system and purify the liver.

LEMON ESSENTIAL OIL

Massage onto the skin in a vegetable oil base to alleviate any congested lymph glands. Inhaled, it has been shown to reduce blood pressure. It also reduces water retention and increases mineral absorption and can be helpful in achieving weight loss. Incorporated into cosmetics, the oil is most effective on oily complexions, clearing acne, blackheads, and other skin impurities.

AROMATHERAPY

Research has proven that the aroma of lemon oil can enhance your mood, and relax you. It is excellent for lifting spirits and effective in a sick room where the patient has had to remain for days at a time, brightening energy and lifting the spirits.

HEARTBURN

Drink a teaspoon of lemon juice in half a glass of water.

RHEUMATISM

3 times a day, consume 25ml to 50ml of lemon juice diluted in water, 1 hour before meals and at bedtime.

HAEMORRHAGE

Drink some lemon juice diluted in very cold water to help curb it.

SCURVY

Eliminated by drinking 1 to 2 ounces of lemon juice diluted with some water every 2–4 hours.

EXCESSIVE MENSTRUATION (MENORRHAGIA)

Swallow the juice of 3–4 lemons a day, each lemon diluted in a glass of cool water.

AGE SPOTS

Squeeze lemon juice onto age spots regularly to fade them, or mix the juice of 1 lemon, 1 lime, 2 tablespoons honey, and 2–4 tablespoons plain yogurt and massage into the skin.

PREVENT SUNBURN

Lemon juice applied onto your skin can help.

LIGHTEN DISCOLOURED ELBOWS

Cut a lemon in half and put one elbow in each half for roughly 10 minutes.

EXFOLIATE DEAD SKIN ON THE FACE

Rub a cut lemon and ½ teaspoon of sugar granules over the skin for a few minutes.

HANGOVER CURE

Rub lemon slices under your armpits! The theory says lemon juice helps you retain fluid that guards against dehydration, whilst balancing the pH levels in your body, as well as replacing the potentially lost vitamin C, thus staving off hangover headaches. Or if you feel a bit silly doing that, you could always reduce your hangover by substituting sugar and milk in your coffee with several drops of fresh lemon juice; sip slowly.

ATHLETE'S FOOT

Combine lemon juice with papaya juice and apply to the affected area.

NOSE BLEED

Put a drop or two of lemon juice in the nostril that is bleeding.

INSECT BITES

Instantly take the sting out with lemon juice. To repel insects, add 20 drops of lemon oil to 250ml water and spray into the air. It smells great and repels insects at the same time. Another home remedy is to place a cotton ball soaked in lemon oil in your bedroom. If you are sitting outside in the evening, apply lemon oil to skin areas not covered in clothing. Or, add 15 drops of lemon oil to 70ml of olive oil and rub into the skin.

Lemon oil has pain-relieving qualities, so to inhibit inflammation and ease pain, massage the affected area daily with 10 drops of lemon oil mixed with 20ml jojoba oil.

BLEEDING GUMS

When massaged gently into gums, lemon juice can help to stop gums bleeding and also calm inflammation of the tongue.

CHAPPED LIPS

Combine lemon juice with glycerine and apply to lips for a natural effective cure.

CUTS

Apply lemon juice to disinfect them and promote healing.

FOR NERVES

Lemons act as a sedative for the nerves, as well as aiding the heart by reducing troublesome palpitations. Drink the juice of 1 lemon mixed with a cup of water.

ABDOMINAL DISTURBANCES

Drinking lemon juice gives immediate relief.

ECZEMA

Mix lemon juice with olive oil to treat it. Another possible treatment is 2 drops of lemon oil patted on using a wet sponge. A lemon wrap may offer relief. Mix 10 drops of lemon oil with 300ml lukewarm water and 20ml of liquid honey. Honey also has anti-inflammatory effects and accentuates the healing abilities of lemon. Soak a linen cloth in the mixture, squeeze out the excess, and gently put the cloth on the affected area, leaving for 20 minutes, 3 times a day. Not only will this ease the infection, it will counter the overwhelming urge to scratch. It has even been reported to calm itchiness in the skin's reaction to poison ivy.

DIABETES RELIEF

Lemon juice mixed with water is effective in quenching the thirst of patients suffering from diabetes.

HEALTH OF TEETH AND BONES

The vitamin C content of lemon helps considerably in calcium metabolism, for example some sources claim consuming lemon juice could prevent osteoarthritis. Whiten your teeth and strengthen the enamel by sucking on a lemon. Wait 30 minutes before brushing your teeth, to give the saliva a chance to neutralise the acid. Brushing your teeth is important to thoroughly remove any residue of acid from the lemon and to protect your tooth enamel.

HAIR CONDITIONER

Mix the juice of 1 lemon with 250ml warm water and apply to hair. Leave on for a few minutes, then rinse. This will add fresh bounce and shine. Or, combine 200ml olive oil, 125ml honey, and 3 tablespoons of lemon juice. Set aside. After shampooing your hair, towel dry and work the lemon juice mixture in your hair by combing it evenly throughout. Cover hair with a plastic cap for half an hour. Shampoo and rinse as usual.

DANDRUFF CARE

Mix a few tablespoons of fresh lemon juice with warm olive oil and rub into the scalp. Leave for 15 minutes, then shampoo and rinse. After shampooing, rinse your hair with water and lemon juice to prevent dandruff and remove soap residue.

GREASY HAIR

Lemon juice is an excellent treatment for greasy hair; simply add a few drops to your normal shampoo.

FOOT CARE

In a foot bath, combine 250ml lemon juice, 2 tablespoons olive oil, 65ml milk, with enough water to fill the footbath. Soak the feet for 15 minutes, then rinse with warm water. Regular use produces noticeably softer, smoother feet.

ASTRINGENT TONER FOR OILY SKIN

Combine 2 tablespoons lemon juice, 2 tablespoons vodka, 1 tablespoon distilled water, 1 teaspoon witch hazel. Apply with cotton wool to skin, then rinse. Follow with a non-comedogenic moisturiser. This will keep for a week if kept in a screw-top bottle in the fridge.

NAILS

Soak your nails in lemon juice for 10 minutes, then brush your nails with a tooth brush or nail brush using a mixture of 1 part white vinegar and 1 part warm water. Rinse with warm water. This treatment helps your fingernails stay strong and bright! Another top lemony nail tip helps nails that have been covered with nail polish for a long time and are now somewhat stained. To remove the stain, simply clean the nails with lemon juice.

BLACKHEADS

Rub lemon juice over the areas that contain blackheads before you go to bed. Rinse your face with cool water when you wake up. Repeat this every night until blackheads are dissolved and gone.

BRIGHTEN SKIN

Use fresh lemon juice on any area of your skin, including your face, before you go to bed, rinse in the morning to reveal brighter and softer skin. You can also add the juice of 4 lemons to your bath water and soak for 20 minutes for an all-over treatment.

BREATH FRESHENER

Lemon has been used for decades as a natural breath-freshener. The acidity in lemons, although alkalising, helps destroy bacteria in your mouth that gives you bad breath. Drink lemon water during the day, or squirt a few drops directly on to your tongue and gargle to freshen your breath! Chewing on a lemon slice after every meal will also help.

LEMON HONEY

Combine lemon and honey in equal measures, apply to the face and leave for 10 minutes. Rinse to reveal glowing skin.

WANT BABY SOFT SKIN? LET LEMONS COME TO THE RESCUE WITH THIS SKIN SCRUB RECIPE

Mix 125g sugar with finely chopped lemon rind and enough olive oil to make a paste. Wet your body in the shower, turn off the water and massage the sugar mix all over. Rinse and relish your newly softened skin.

CYSTITIS CURE

Lemon will help to kill bacteria in the bladder and stop the burning sensation felt during urination. It will also reduce any bleeding. Add fresh lemon juice to water and drink as much as possible. Barley, which is high in alkalinity, will also reduce the acidity present in the urine, and is also known to help ease the side effects of cystitis, so drink lemon barley water (see recipe for Lemon Barley Drink on p.69).

DETOXIFIER

Lemon water is a great purifier for your body, simply sip warm or cool water with lemon juice in it throughout the day.

ACNE

Help to fight and prevent acne by mixing one part freshly squeezed lemon juice with an equal part of rose water. Spread onto the affected areas and leave for at least half an hour. Afterwards remove with water. Repeat twice daily, ideally in the morning and evening.

Applied with a cotton ball, a little lemon juice acts as an astringent, eliminating oil and tightening the pores for a smoother look. Mix salt and lemon juice into a paste for an all natural exfoliant.

LEMON BALM

Melissa is the botanical name for this herb, the Greek word for 'bee'. Lemon balm has been cultivated in the Mediterranean region for around 2,000 years. The Muslim herbalist Avicenna suggested lemon balm 'to make the heart merry'. Paracelsus claimed the herb could completely rejuvenate the body, calling it the 'elixir of life', whilst 14th century French King Charles V drank lemon balm tea every day to maintain his health. During the 17th century Carmelite nuns invented Carmelite Water, which treated nerves, headaches and neuralgia. The water was a combination of lemon balm with lemon rind, nutmeg, coriander and angelica root. The herb has been recorded as being sacred to the temple of Diana and in Southern Europe, the balm was named 'heart's delight'. Renowned for lifting the spirits, it has been eulogised by herbalists for centuries. Today it is not uncommon for lemon balm to be used in aromatherapy to defy depression. Lemon Balm has been employed in the pursuit of love. It is a magnetising herb which has been known to be made into a charm and worn to attract a lover into someone's life. The scented leaves can be scattered in a bath to exude romance.

ANAEMIA

Lemon essential oil because of its vitamin C content is beneficial for treating anaemia.

VARICOSE VEINS

Lemon oil has been reported to strengthen vascular tissues, therefore it can be used for treating varicose and spider veins by improving circulation and relieving pressure on the veins. It may be applied in skin lotions and compresses, mixed in a 1:1 ratio with Cypress essential oil, jojoba, avocado or almond oil.

IMMUNE SYSTEM

Lemon essential oil is an excellent stimulant of the body's own immune system. It activates white blood cell formation and helps protect the body during flu epidemics.

CELLULITE

Take several drops of lemon essential oil and rub on cellulite to improve circulation and help eliminate waste from the cells.

CHOLESTERAL

Pectin power in lemons along with its other metabolism and circulation boosting nutrients can help lower cholesterol. Lemon juice lowers blood pressure and increases the level of HDL (good cholesterol).

FATIGUE

Long distance walkers, world travellers, and explorers look upon the lemon as a godsend. When fatigue sets in, they can suck on a lemon by piercing the top of the fruit with a straw, giving themselves a quick-acting medication and lovely refreshment. Explorers also use lemon for protection against many tropical infections. A small amount of lemon juice will quench thirst more effectively than the same amount of water. Experienced travellers assert that when they add lemon juice to ordinary drinking water, it acts as an antiseptic and prevents illness due to adverse reactions to the water supplies.

Lemon oil also seems to be able to stimulate brain activity so whenever you feel tired or are finding it hard to focus or concentrate, add 4 drops of lemon oil to a water-filled aromatherapy lamp. Alternatively, drink a glass of lemon water every few hours.

PORTABLE STRESS RELIEF

If you feel tense, sprinkle a few drops of lemon balm essential oil (Melissa officinalis) onto a handkerchief and inhale deeply.

INFECTION

Lemon juice fights against infection, whilst helping the production of white blood cells and antibodies to attack the invading micro-organism, thus preventing infection.

HEADACHE

Dried and ground lemon rind when massaged into the scalp for a few minutes before a bath, can relieve a nasty headache, whilst cooling the body.

WEIGHT LOSS

Drinking lemon juice with a pinch of salt every morning in warm water lowers cholesterol and helps weight loss. It also helps your body optimise the energy from the food you eat.

DIMINISH WRINKLES

30g	**plain yogurt**
1 tbsp	**runny honey**
½	**lemon, juice only**
	Liquid from 4 pure vitamin E capsules

Mix the ingredients, apply to your face, leave for 15 minutes and rinse.

LEMON BARLEY DRINK

Here is a recipe that combines both lemon and barley to ease the pain of cystitis.

2	**organic unwaxed lemons**
125g	**pearl barley**
1½ltr	**boiling water**

Finely grate lemon zest from both lemons into a saucepan. Rinse the pearl barley and add to the saucepan with the boiling water, simmer for 20 minutes. Stir well and leave to cool. Squeeze the juice from the lemons and mix into the cooled barley water. Strain through a sieve and chill.

LEMON & EGG SHAMPOO

Revitalises and nourishes your hair, making it look shiny and feel super soft, without any possible harmful chemicals that might be present in commercially made shampoos.

1	**egg**
45ml	**unscented shampoo**
1	**lemon, juice only**
15ml	**lemon essence**

Mix all the ingredients together in a bowl until blended. Apply the mixture to your hair like a normal shampoo and massage well. Rinse off with water.

A MODERN TWIST ON A 17TH CENTURY ENGLISH CAWDLE (A SOOTHING LEMON & EGG DRINK) FOR A POORLY PERSON

600ml	**double cream**
150g	**caster sugar**
	Pinch ground cinnamon
	Drop vanilla extract
6	**egg yolks**
2	**large lemons, zest & juice**

Put all ingredients except the egg yolks, juice and lemon zest into a large pan over a low heat and gradually bring to the boil. Boil for 3 minutes, then remove from the heat, beat in the egg yolks and allow to cool. Add the lemon juice and zest and whisk well. Serve.

SUGARING IS A METHOD OF EPILATION SIMILAR TO WAXING

200g	**sugar**
8	**lemons, juice only**
250ml	**water**
1	**wooden spatula**
	Strips of cotton fabric*

In a pan, over a medium heat, combine and stir together the ingredients until well mixed. It should be a pale yellow, remove from the heat before it darkens too much. Allow the liquid to cool to room temperature. Use a wooden spatula to spread the mixture over the areas to be waxed. Lay the strips of cotton fabric over the mixture, rub down firmly and swiftly tear the strip away. It will remove the sugar mixture and the hair, leaving the skin clean.

*how many depends on how big the area is that you intend on waxing.

LEMON CONDITIONING FACE MASK

30ml	**sour cream**
20g	**raw porridge oats**
½	**lemon, juice only**

Mix all the ingredients in a bowl, and pat onto your face, avoiding the eye area. Leave for 10 minutes then rinse off with warm water.

LEMON ANTIOXIDANT FACE MASK

80ml	**olive oil**
60g	**powdered clay**
16 drops	**lemon essential oil**

In a bowl, combine the olive oil, powdered clay and lemon essential oil. Apply to the face, avoiding the eye area. Leave for 20 minutes, and then rinse off with warm water. Wash off immediately, if skin irritation occurs.

LEMONY DRINK RECIPES

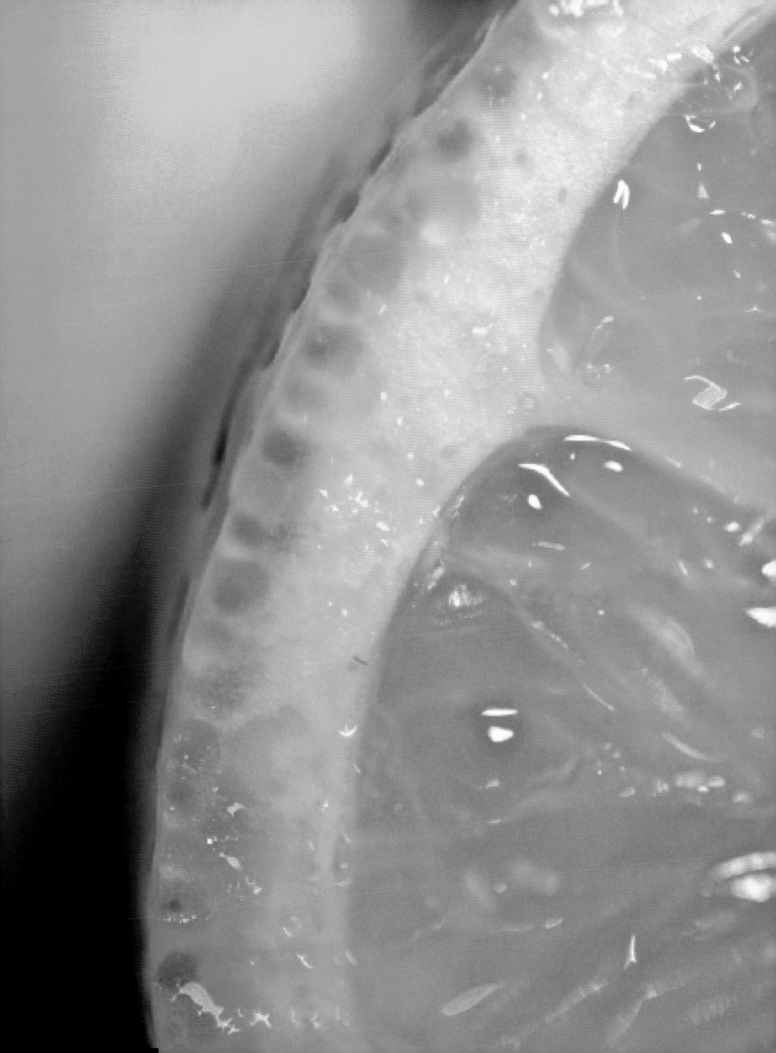

ALCOHOLIC

GIN & LEMON

45ml	**gin**
15ml	**lemon juice**
½ tsp	**caster sugar**
125ml	**tonic water**
	ice cubes

In a shaker half-filled with ice cubes, combine the gin, lemon juice and sugar. Shake well. Strain into a glass, almost filled to the top with ice cubes. Top up with the tonic water and serve.

STREGA COCKTAIL

I was given a bottle of Liquore Strega at an Italian event, and shortly after made up this refreshing drink. Strega is an Italian herbal liqueur devised during the sixties in one of my favourite regions of Italy; Campania. Its unique recipe includes around 70 herbs, including mint and fennel, with saffron producing the yellow colour.

Serves 1

30ml	**Liquore Strega**
200ml	**tonic water**
1	**lemon, juice only**
2–3	**ice cubes**

Simply mix all the ingredients together, drop a few ice cubes into your favourite glass and serve.

BLACK LEMON COCKTAIL

Simple and delicious.

45ml	**chocolate liqueur**
30ml	**Limoncello**
2–3	**ice cubes**

Pour ingredients over the ice cubes in a chilled cocktail glass. Stir and serve.

GIN & LEMON

EIERPUNSCH (EGG PUNCH)

Warm, sweet, alcoholic, egg-based drink, not unlike eggnog. Seen everywhere during Christmas. Enjoy...

Serves 4

125ml	**strong tea**
4¼ tbsp	**brown sugar**
2	**eggs**
400ml	**white wine**
2 tsp	**vanilla extract**
½ tsp	**allspice**
2	**cloves**
½ tsp	**cinnamon**
½ tsp	**nutmeg**
½	**lemon, juice only**

Make the tea and leave to cool. With an electric hand-held whisk, beat together the sugar and eggs, add 10ml of wine, whisk again. Add the vanilla extract, remaining wine, allspice, cloves, cinnamon, nutmeg, lemon juice and tea.

Transfer the mixture to a saucepan and whisk continuously over a medium heat (do not allow to come to the boil), until the liquid has thickened, about 5 minutes. Do not let the mixture heat too quickly. Remove from the heat, before the mixture comes to the boil, it should be foaming on top. Discard the cloves. Serve hot with your favourite biscuit, shown opposite with a Roman Biscuit (p.194).

SPARKLING WINE LEMON SORBET

Known in Spain as 'Sorbete de Cava y Limon' and in Italy as 'Sgroppino', a traditional Venetian treat.

Serves 3–4

1ltr	**good quality lemon sorbet/ice cream**
1	**bottle of sparkling wine, chilled (Cava)**
3–4	**strawberries**

Remove the sorbet from the freezer and allow to soften for about 10 minutes. Put half of the sorbet into a blender, pouring half of the sparkling wine over it, blend well. Put in the rest of the wine and sorbet blend until frothy.

Decant into chilled wine glasses and garnish each glass with a fresh strawberry. Serve immediately.

CHAMPAGNE LIMONCELLO COCKTAIL

Serves 8

1	**lemon wedge, for glass rims**
4 tbsp	**sugar**
8	**lemon rind strips**
8 tbsp	**Limoncello**
4 tsp	**fresh lemon juice**
1	**bottle Champagne, chilled**

Sugar the glass rims by rubbing a cut lemon wedge around the rim of each glass, then dip in sugar. Next, roll up the strips of lemon rind and place one into each of the champagne flutes. Add 1 tbsp Limoncello and ½ tsp juice to each glass. Divide champagne evenly among glasses. Serve immediately.

PALÜZE

A yummy drink recipe given by an experimental Cypriot barman, who took a combination of the local drink Brandy Sour and a local grape-based pudding: Palüze, as inspiration.

Serves 1

9	**red grapes**
50ml	**Three Barrels VSOP**
25ml	**lemon juice**
25ml	**sugar syrup**
1	**mint sprig**
	Crushed ice

Place 5 grapes with the rest of the ingredients in a cocktail shaker and give it a good shake! Pour into a highball glass half filled with crushed ice. Garnish with 4 grapes on a toothpick and a mint sprig on top.

LEMON DROP

Serves 1

	Ice cubes
45ml	**vodka**
20ml	**lemon juice**
1 tsp	**sugar syrup**
	Lemon twist, for garnish

Place ice cubes in a cocktail shaker. Add the vodka, lemon juice and sugar syrup. Shake well. Strain into a chilled cocktail glass. Garnish with the lemon twist.

CHAMPAGNE LIMONCELLO COCKTAIL

LEMON LAVENDER PUNCH

Lavender and lemon are a love match made in heaven. In June, July and August fresh lavender is widely available.

700g	**seedless black grapes**
35g	**lavender flowers**
110g	**caster sugar**
320ml	**water**
1	**cinnamon stick**
10	**cloves**
2	**lemons, juice only**
⅓	**bottle of your favourite claret**
1	**bottle Rosé Champagne**
Garnish	
1	**lemon, finely sliced**

Purée the grapes in a blender. Add this to the lavender, sugar, water, cinnamon and cloves. Transfer to a saucepan and bring to the boil. Reduce the heat and simmer for 8 minutes. Combine with the lemon juice and claret when cool. Pour into a container, seal tightly and refrigerate overnight.

When you are ready to serve, combine with the Rosé, stir and distribute between your glasses, garnishing with a lemon slice. Enjoy.

TEA & CITRUS FRUIT PUNCH

1ltr	**cooled black tea (use 4 tea bags)**
500ml	**orange juice**
300ml	**fresh lemon juice**
360ml	**rum**
150ml	**cherry brandy**
50g	**caster sugar**
	Crushed ice
	Lemon slices, for garnish

To make this very easy adult party drink, combine all ingredients in a punch bowl. Simply pour into glasses filled with crushed ice, dress with a lemon slice.

PLANTERS PUNCH

For my Planters Punch I chose a mixture of pineapple and coconut but you could play around with your preference of taste, mango would also work wonderfully...

700ml	**dark rum**
700ml	**pure cane syrup**
45ml	**angostura bitters**
1ltr	**pineapple & coconut juice**
12	**lemons, juice only**
	Ice cubes

Combine and mix all ingredients except the ice, pour into a punch bowl. Serve in glasses over ice.

LOVELY LIME, LIMONCELLO & LEMON COCKTAIL

150ml	**tonic water**
30ml	**brandy**
½	**lemon, juice only**
½	**lime, juice only**
30ml	**Limoncello**
3	**basil leaves, finely shredded**
	Ice cubes

Mix together all of the ingredients, except the ice cubes, either in a cocktail shaker or in a glass. Give it a good stir and then drop in the ice cubes.

RUM PUNCH

As I made this punch with some friends, we did all think it would be incredibly sweet, virtually feeling our teeth disintegrate as we poured the sugar cane syrup in, but it was surprisingly not as sweet as we thought and rather delicious, hence its inclusion...

700ml	**dark rum**
700ml	**pure cane syrup**
45ml	**angostura bitters**
12	**lemons, juice only**
	Ice cubes

Combine and mix all ingredients except the ice, pour into a punch bowl. Serve in glasses over ice.

HOME-MADE LIMONCELLO

This recipe was given to me by Villa Massa, producers of Limoncello in Sorrento, Italy, after I had visited their gorgeous and tranquil premises one October...

10	**large lemons**
1ltr	**pure alcohol (95%)**
1½ltr	**water**
1·2kg	**sugar**

Wash the lemons in warm water and discard any residue. Peel them with a potato peeler, cutting away the external part of the peel (the pith should remain attached to the lemons, as it tastes very bitter).
Put the peels on a cutting board and slice them into matchstick strips. Add them with 750ml of the alcohol to a large, sterilised glass container (jar or jug) with a tight-fitting lid or cap, close and leave to macerate for one month, in a cool, dark place.

After one month, boil the water and add the sugar, stirring until dissolved. Leave this syrup to cool. When cold add it to the glass container with the infused peel and the rest of the alcohol. Close the container and leave it for another 40 days, still in a cool, dark place. After 40 days, open the container, strain the liqueur into frost-proof bottles and place in the freezer. The home-made Limoncello is ready to be tasted.

NON-ALCOHOLIC

LEMON, GINGER & ROOIBOS TEA

Serves 1

1 tbsp	**honey**
2·5cm	**ginger, thinly sliced**
5–10	**cloves**
250ml	**hot water**
1	**Rooibos teabag**
1	**lemon, juice only**

Couldn't be easier – put it all in a glass then stir.

LEMON ICED TEA

200ml	**strong tea**
120ml	**cold water**
2	**lemons, juice only**
	Sugar, to taste
120ml	**crushed ice**
2	**sprigs fresh mint**
1	**slice lemon**

Combine the tea, water, lemon juice and sugar and chill for at least 1 hour in the fridge. Pour into glasses filled with crushed ice, garnish with mint sprigs and a slice of lemon.

LEMON, GINGER & ROOIBOS TEA

ROSY CHEEKS

Sharp, sweet and floral, the perfect way to get your daily dose of lemon juice...

Serves 1

150ml	**fresh orange juice**
150ml	**fresh pomegranate juice**
125ml	**lemon juice**
2 drops	**rose water**
	Ice cubes

Pour all the liquids into a cocktail shaker or directly into a pint glass, make sure they are well combined, drop in a few ice cubes if desired and serve.

WARM MINT & LEMON

This soothing herbal drink is thought to calm an upset stomach and reduce stress.

Serves 4

1	**lemon**
30g	**fresh mint leaves**
1ltr	**boiling water**

Making sure not to incorporate any of the white pith, peel the lemon. Put the rind, mint leaves and boiling water in a bowl, cover and leave for 5 minutes. Strain mixture through a fine sieve. Serve immediately.

COCONUT & LEMON QUENCHER

Both ingredients are amazing natural hydrators...

200ml	**coconut water**
½	**lemon, juice only**

Get a glass, pour both the juices in, stir, drink!

LEMON COOLER

To prepare your frosted glasses, rub a cut lemon wedge around the rim of each glass, then dip into caster sugar.

2	**lemons**
225g	**caster sugar**
225g	**crushed ice**
1ltr	**water**
2 tbsp	**rosewater**

Extract the juice from the lemons and set aside. In a bowl combine sugar, crushed ice, water, lemon juice and rosewater, stir. When the sugar is completely dissolved, strain and serve in frosted glasses.

GRANITA DI LIMONE (LEMON ICE)

This takes me right back to the Amalfi Coast, enthusiastically sipping, with the sun soaking my bones, as I wait for the boat...

Serves 2

400ml	**water**
170g	**sugar**
1	**large lemon, juice & zest**

In a saucepan bring to a boil the water and sugar. Simmer for a few minutes until the sugar has dissolved. Remove from the heat and add the lemon juice and zest. Transfer to a freezable container large enough to hold the liquid and leave to cool.

Once cool, freeze for a total of 4 hours, breaking up the mixture with a fork at least once every hour. It will then be ready to serve in your favourite glass any time you fancy a refreshing treat.

WATERMELON, LEMON & ROSEMARY SLURP

MA'S LEMONADE

WATERMELON, LEMON & ROSEMARY SLURP

500ml	water
185g	caster sugar
2	sprigs rosemary stripped and chopped
18	lemons, juice only
1	medium watermelon, de-seeded and cubed
	Ice cubes

Over a high heat bring the water and sugar to a boil in a saucepan. Stir in the rosemary, and set aside to steep for 1 hour. Place the lemon juice with the watermelon in a blender.

Strain the rosemary syrup through a mesh strainer into the blender, puree until smooth. Refrigerate until very cold, give it a good stir before serving over ice.

MA'S LEMONADE

1	lemon
4	sugar lumps
300ml	boiling water

Strip the rind from the lemon using a potato peeler, being careful not to incorporate any pith. Put the rind, the juice of the lemon and the sugar in a jug and pour the boiling water over them. Cover closely and when cool, strain and drink.

LIMEY LEMON

Serves 8

1ltr	lime soda
14	lemons, juice only
4	limes, juice only
8	slices lemon
8	slices lime

In a bowl, combine all liquids. Pour into 8 glasses garnished with a slice each of lemon and lime, serve.

LEMON MINT CUCUMBER

One of my favourite drinks all year round, but particularly feels clean and fresh sliding down your throat on a hot summer day! Also makes a very attractive variation on the dinner table in place of water.

1	**cucumber, sliced**
1	**lemon, sliced**
	Small handful fresh mint leaves
2ltr	**water**

Combine the cucumber, lemon and mint in a jug. Fill with water and leave in the fridge for 30 minutes for the flavours to infuse.

LEMON & GINGER TEA

320ml	**black tea**
40g	**ginger, crystallised, finely chopped**
1	**lemon, thinly sliced**
650ml	**ginger beer**

Combine tea, ginger and half the lemon slices in a saucepan, bring to a boil, turn off heat and set aside. When it has cooled, strain through a fine sieve into a jug. Add in the ginger beer. Put the rest of the lemon slices into the jug, stir, refrigerate for at least half an hour. Serve cold.

LEMON MYRTLE

6	**lemon myrtle leaves**
	Boiling water
2ltr	**mineral water**

Steep the leaves in just enough boiling water to cover and set aside to cool for around an hour, the colour of the water should have darkened. Add to the mineral water, stir and serve.

LEMON MINT CUCUMBER

LEMON & GINGER TEA

PINK LEMONADE

250g	**caster sugar**
240ml	**water**
240ml	**cranberry juice**
240ml	**lemon juice**

Heat sugar and water in a saucepan and cook until the sugar is completely dissolved. Remove from the heat. Stir together with the cranberry juice and lemon juice. Chill for 1 hour at least, before serving mixed with sparkling water.

NIMBU SQUASH

Optional and traditional garnishes would include fresh mint leaves, sprinkles of table salt or a pinch of black salt (Kala Namak).

225g	**caster sugar**
250ml	**water**
3	**lemons, juice only**
15ml	**vinegar**

In a saucepan over a medium heat, dissolve the sugar in the water. Remove from the heat and cool. Combine the sugar water with the lemon juice and vinegar and transfer to a jug. Pop into the fridge, serve cold.

ASIAN INSPIRED LEMONADE (JAL JEERA PANI)

4	**lemons, juice only**
	Enough water to fill a large jug
	Sugar or honey, to taste
2 tbsp	**Jaljira powder***
	Crushed ice
	Lemon slices, for garnish

Squeeze the lemons, strain the juice and pour into a large jug. Fill the jug with water, sweeten to taste, add the jaljira powder, stir and add crushed ice. Serve in chilled glasses, topping with a lemon slice.

*normally in Asian markets and generally consists of cumin, ginger, black pepper, mint, black salt, some fruit powder; usually either mango, or some kind of citrus zest and chilli.

CANARINO

Scrummy and simple classic Italian beverage.

1	**lemon, rind only, no pith**
	Pot hot water

Traditionally canarino (little canary) is made by using a whole pared lemon rind steeped in a pot of hot water. Its flavour comes from a blend of natural lemon oils and acids in the lemon rind. Sugar or honey can be added to enhance the flavour to taste. For a summer version, pour chilled canarino over ice. For a cocktail, add vodka, gin, or a splash of vermouth.

LEMON VERBENA

1ltr	**mineral water**
3	**sprigs lemon verbena**
	Handful fresh mint leaves
4 tbsp	**honey**

Bring the water to the boil in a saucepan and remove from the heat. Stir in the lemon verbena, mint and honey. Infuse for 10 minutes, strain, pop into the fridge and serve cold.

YELLOW FRUIT SLUSH

YELLOW FRUIT SLUSH

Everyone seems to love this!

2	**lemons, juice & zest**
2	**oranges, juice & zest**
½	**fresh pineapple, cut into chunks**
200g	**sugar**
500ml	**ginger beer**
4	**bananas**

In a blender, blitz all ingredients until smooth. Transfer to a freezable container and pop into the freezer overnight. Allow to thaw for 10 minutes before serving in a glass with a spoon.

CALCIUM COOLER

A refreshing and super healthy drink, full of calcium from the yogurt and the almonds...

Serves 1

Glass rim

½	**lemon**
1 tbsp	**ground almond**

Drink

1	**lemon ½ juice, 1 zest**
150g	**plain organic yogurt**
150ml	**almond milk**
1 tsp	**caster sugar**
1 drop	**orange extract**
1 drop	**almond extract**
1 cup	**ice cubes**

Begin by rubbing half the lemon around the rim of a pint glass. Pour the ground almonds onto a shallow dish and dip the rim of the glass into it, covering well. Place all of the drink ingredients into a blender except the ice, once combined, pour over some ice cubes in your almond rimmed glass, yum.

LEMONY SAVOURY RECIPES

LEMONY GLUTEN-FREE SPAGHETTI

Quick and easy, a great dish for anyone following a gluten-free diet...

Serves 2

180g	**spaghetti, gluten-free**
2	**courgettes**
1 tbsp	**olive oil**
1 tsp	**chilli flakes**
2	**lemons, zest only**
2 tbsp	**pine nuts**

First, cook the gluten-free spaghetti as per the packet instructions. Grate the courgettes and squeeze in a muslin cloth to expel the excess liquid.

In a large frying pan, fry the grated courgettes in the olive oil, with the chilli flakes, lemon zest and pine nuts. Add the spaghetti to the frying pan and stir until it is coated by the chilli mixture. Serve.

PORK MEDALLIONS WITH GRUYÈRE & LEMON SAUCE

With your choice of veg and perhaps (as I do) with some baked apple slices.

Serves 3

6	**pork medallions**
100g	**fresh breadcrumbs**
2	**lemons, zest only**
10	**fresh rosemary leaves, chopped**
1 tsp	**wholegrain mustard**
	Pinch salt & pepper
50g	**plain flour**
100ml	**milk**
2	**free range eggs**
1 tbsp	**olive oil**
1 tbsp	**butter**
Gruyère & Lemon Sauce	
100g	**butter**
2	**lemons, juice only**
100g	**Gruyère cheese**

Using a meat mallet or a rolling pin, beat the medallions until thinned out to about 5mm. Combine the breadcrumbs in a bowl with lemon zest, rosemary, mustard, salt and pepper. Knead well with your fingers.

Sift the flour into a separate bowl. In another bowl, mix together the milk and eggs. Now, pat one of the pork medallions into the flour, next dip it into the egg mixture, and coat in the breadcrumbs. Dip and coat the medallion a second time, ensuring it is well covered. Place on a plate and repeat with the remaining medallions.

Put the olive oil and butter into a large frying pan, over a medium heat, melt the two together. When the butter foams, add the medallions, frying until golden on each side. When they are completely cooked through, remove from the pan and drain on kitchen paper. Cover to keep warm.

For the sauce, in a saucepan over a medium heat, combine and melt together the butter and lemon juice with the cheese, stirring continuously with a balloon whisk until a sauce texture emerges. Serve the medallions with a generous scoop of the sauce.

LEMONY GLUTEN-FREE SPAGHETTI

SALMON STEAKS WITH TAHINI & LEMON SAUCE

Fish served with a tahini sauce is a firm favourite throughout the Middle East, called samak bi tahini in Arabic. I like to serve my salmon interpretation alongside some steaming rice...

Serves 2

5 tbsp	olive oil
2	large salmon fillets
3 tbsp	tahini paste
1	lemon, juice & zest
½	orange, juice
1	clove garlic, finely sliced
1 tbsp	olive oil
	Salt & black pepper
1	small red onion, thinly sliced

Preheat the oven to 220°C/425°F/Gas 7. Brush 4 tablespoons of the olive oil over the fish, put into a shallow oven dish and cook for 10 minutes. Make the sauce by combining the remaining ingredients except the onion in a bowl, set aside. Remove salmon from the oven, cover with the sauce and a layer of onion slices, then return to the oven for another 10 minutes. The fish is cooked when it flakes easily using the tip of a fork.

COD WITH A PRESERVED LEMON & PISTACHIO CRUST

A tasty way to jazz up a cod fillet, serve with your favourite veg and perhaps roast potatoes.

Serves 2

	Pinch salt
40g	unsalted pistachios, shelled
1 tbsp	capers
2	preserved lemons*
½	fresh red chilli, deseeded, finely sliced
80ml	extra virgin olive oil, & more for finishing
	Large handful flat leaf parsley, leaves only
2	cod fillets
1	lemon, cut in wedges

Preheat the oven to 200°C/400°F/Gas 6. Combine and mix well in a food blender the salt, pistachios, capers, preserved lemon rind and fresh chilli, when in a paste, add 60ml olive oil and lastly parsley – blend briefly once more. Transfer the fish to an oven dish, divide the preserved lemon mixture evenly onto both, pressing lightly so it adheres well to the fillets. Pour enough water in the dish around the fish, so it comes halfway up the sides of the fillets, place in the oven.

Bake for 15 minutes or until firm and cooked through. Before you serve, garnish with a drizzle of olive oil (20ml), put a couple of lemon wedges on each – done.

*Pith and flesh removed and discarded.

STUFFED LEMONS

This dish, ideal as a starter, was inspired by a recipe found regularly along the Amalfi coast (lemon heaven)! in Italy, called limoni cotti al forno. Delicious served with sumptuous bread to mop up all the juices.

Serves 4

4	rashers smoked bacon, cut into 4 pieces each
4	large lemons
16	mini mozerella balls (250g)
16	fresh basil leaves
8	cherry tomatoes, sliced into 3
1	fresh red chilli, deseeded, 16 thin slices
8 tsp	olive oil
	Pinch salt & pepper

Preheat the oven to 200°C/400°F/Gas 6. In a saucepan, dry fry the bacon pieces until crisp, turn the heat off and set aside. Top and tail the lemons, without cutting any of the flesh inside. Cut the lemons in half, leaving 2 even sized halves. Use a pairing knife to remove the flesh, so you have 8 hollow 'lemon cups'.

Place a mini mozzarella ball in the base of each cup, followed by 2 basil leaves, 3 slices of cherry tomato, 2 chilli slices, 2 bacon pieces, 1 tsp of olive oil, pinch of salt & pepper and finished with a mini mozzarella ball, press down to fit cup. Arrange the lemon cups in a shallow roasting pan and bake for 10–15 minutes, when ready, they will be bubbling and the cheese will be golden.

LUSCIOUS LEMONY LINGUINE

Serves 2

200g	linguine
80g	asparagus, chopped
60g	frozen peas
3	spring onions, chopped
3 tbsp	olive oil
1	lemon, juice & zest
1	clove garlic, minced
	Pinch salt & pepper

Cook the linguine according to the packet instructions in a large pan. Five minutes or so before the end of cooking time, add the asparagus and peas into the pan. Drain and return to the pan. Add the rest of the ingredients, except the zest, stir with a spoon. Dish up and sprinkle the zest over the top (as you would parmesan). Serve immediately.

HALLOUMI & PRESERVED LEMON RELISH

A lonely packet of halloumi was in the fridge, lightly crisp in some olive oil, yes, but with what...

3 tbsp	**olive oil**
250g	**block halloumi, cut into 10 slices**

Preserved Lemon Relish

1	**lemon, juice & zest**
3 tbsp	**olive oil**
2	**preserved lemon, pulp removed, rind sliced finely**
15	**cherry tomatoes, quartered**
½ tsbp	**runny honey**
1 tsp	**capers, rinsed**
7·5cm	**cucumber, diced**
2	**spring onions, finely sliced**
	Pinch salt & pepper
	Small bunch fresh coriander leaves

To make this easy snack or delicious starter, in a large frying pan heat the olive oil, crisp the halloumi on both sides until golden brown.

To make the preserved lemon relish, in a bowl mix all of the remaining ingredients. Serve slices of the halloumi with a scoop of the relish. Bon Appétit.

LEMON SEA BASS EN PAPILLOTE

Tasty with salad and buttered new potatoes.

Serves 1

1	**whole sea bass***
8	**sprigs rosemary**
2	**cloves garlic**
30ml	**olive oil**
½	**onion, sliced**
	Generous pinch fresh parsley, chopped
1	**lemon, sliced**
1	**lemon, juice only**

Preheat the oven to 200°C/400°F/Gas 6. Cut 4 slashes in one side of the fish (not both sides or the yummy juices drain away), taking care not to go right through to the bone. Next, insert the rosemary into the slashes, and another one in the stomach cavity along with the garlic. Drizzle olive oil all over the outside.

Place the fish on a large square of greaseproof paper. Scatter the onion and parsley over the top of the fish. Garnish the fish with the lemon slices. Bring the sides of the paper up over the fish and crimp the paper round the edges, turned in tightly to create a well sealed packet, but leaving a pocket of air inside for it to steam. Cook for about 30 minutes. Before serving, squeeze lemon juice over the fish.

*gutted and de-scaled, skin and head intact

LEMON QUINOA

A light accompaniment to your favourite fish or meat, or indeed meat substitute.

Serves 4

180g	**quinoa**
350ml	**water**
1	**large clove garlic, crushed**
3 tbsp	**tahini**
1	**lemon, juice & zest**
¼	**fresh red chilli**
1 tbsp	**olive oil**
2 tbsp	**hot water**
1 can	**chickpeas, drained**
80g	**feta cheese, cubed**
	Handful coriander leaves, chopped

Rinse the quinoa in a fine meshed sieve. In a saucepan, bring the quinoa and water to a boil. Reduce the heat and simmer until water is fully absorbed, around 15 minutes.

Whilst the quinoa is cooking make the dressing. In a large bowl using a hand-blender, combine the garlic, tahini, lemon zest and juice, chilli pepper and olive oil. Add the hot water to thin it out a little.

When the quinoa is cooked, add to the sauce, along with the chickpeas, feta and coriander leaves. Serve.

ROAST CHESTNUT & MUSHROOM PÂTÉ

On a cool November night, with a bowl of chestnuts screaming to be roasted, a mushroom pâté was born. Delicious served on hot toast, crackers, or I rather like it, as a filling for my sweet potato... Enjoy.

100g	**roasted chestnuts, peeled**
90g	**quark**
400g	**mushrooms**
10g	**unsalted mixed nuts**
1	**lemon, juice & zest**
	Handful fresh coriander leaves
	Pinch salt & pepper
20ml	**water (if needed)**

Put all the ingredients into a blender, blend until smooth. If it is a little thick, add in the water.

LEMON STYLE COUSCOUS

I like to eat this with lamb chops, but it goes well with most meat or fish, as well as being a meal on its own perhaps with some grilled halloumi for the vegetarians out there...

Serves 4

400g	**couscous**
60ml	**olive oil**
2	**lemons, juice only**
400ml	**boiling water**
	Pinch salt & pepper

Pomegranate Garnish

1	**lemon, cut into wedges**
	Handful fresh coriander leaves, chopped
1	**pomegranate, seeds only**

Put all ingredients except the garnish into a bowl. Stir, cover and leave aside for 10 minutes, the couscous will absorb the boiling water and cook. To serve, decorate with the pomegranate garnish.

PRESERVED LEMON & PINK PEPPERCORN CHICKEN THIGHS

1 tbsp	**pink peppercorns, pounded**
2	**lemons, juice only**
2 tbsp	**honey**
1 tbsp	**wholegrain mustard**
4	**cloves garlic, crushed**
6	**large chicken thighs**
4	**preserved lemons, pith & flesh removed, rind sliced finely**
2 tbsp	**capers**
	Large handful fresh flat leaf parsley, chopped

In a bowl, combine the peppercorns, lemon juice, honey, mustard and garlic, mix well. Add the chicken thighs to the mix, turn them around in the sauce to coat well. Transfer the chicken to a roasting pan, pour the excess sauce over the top and set aside to marinate for at least an hour (overnight would be best). When the chicken has marinated, cook in a 200°C/400°F/Gas 6 oven for 45 minutes, turning over after 20 minutes.

When the chicken is golden and cooked all the way through, remove from the oven and sprinkle over the preserved lemon rind, capers and parsley. Toss before serving as desired.

LEMON STYLE COUSCOUS

LEMON INFUSED POTATO SALAD

4	**medium size potatoes, cubed**
Dressing	
	Generous pinch salt & pepper
2	**cloves garlic, crushed**
2 tbsp	**wholegrain mustard**
2	**lemons, juice & zest**
80ml	**olive oil**
6	**spring onions, sliced**

In a saucepan, cook the potatoes in water, over a medium heat, until tender but not mushy, around 15 minutes.

To make the dressing, whisk together the remaining ingredients, except the spring onion. When combined, stir in the spring onion. When the potatoes are cooked, transfer to a serving dish and drizzle over the dressing whilst warm, which will help the flavour infuse. Serve.

LEMONY GREEN BEANS

450g	**fresh green beans**
2	**lemons, juice & zest**
30ml	**olive oil**
	Pinch salt & pepper

Start by topping and tailing the beans. Cook them in a saucepan of water over a medium heat for about 5 minutes, you want them al dente, remove from the heat and set aside. In a bowl, combine the remaining ingredients, stir and pour over the beans. Mix well and serve warm.

LEMON GARLIC BREAD

Tasty indulgent treat!

1	**baguette**
10	**cloves garlic, crushed**
60g	**butter, softened**
2 tbsp	**grated parmesan**
2	**lemons, juice 1, zest 2**
	Pinch pepper

Preheat your oven to 200°C/400°F/Gas 6. Make diagonal slashes in the bread every inch but be careful not to cut all the way through the bread. Mix the other ingredients together, pack it into the gaps between the slashes, using a knife to spread the mixture. Wrap the baguette tightly in a piece of foil and bake for 20 minutes. Serve.

LEMON INFUSED POTATO SALAD

LEMONY GREEN BEANS

LEMON SALMON

LEMON SALMON

Easy supper, delicious served with rice and salad...

Serves 2

2	**salmon steaks**
30ml	**olive oil**
2	**carrots, mini batons**
½	**butternut squash, peeled & sliced into rounds**
1	**lemon, juice & zest**
	Small handful fresh dill, chopped
	Pinch salt & pepper

Preheat the oven to 220°C/425°F/Gas 7. Place each salmon steak in the centre of a square of foil. Top with the remaining ingredients, evenly distributed between the two. Bring the sides of the foil up over the fish and crimp the foil round the edges, turned in tightly to create a well sealed packet, but leaving a pocket of air inside for it to steam. Transfer to a baking tray and bake for 20 minutes. Serve.

ROAST CHESTNUT, BACON & LEMON MEDLEY

Perfect accompaniment to a Sunday roast or as a light lunch topped with a poached egg.

8	**roasted chestnuts**
250g	**brussel sprouts**
4	**rashers smoked bacon, chopped**
15g	**butter**
1 tsp	**olive oil**
1	**lemon, zest & ½ juice**
	Pinch salt & pepper

Roast the chestnuts in a fireplace or oven until blackened, remove, and when cool, peel them and chop each into 4. Cook the sprouts, using the method you normally would but only until al dente, drain, cut in half and reserve aside.

Dry-fry the bacon until crisp in a large frying pan. Remove the bacon from the pan, replace it with the butter and oil. Add the sprouts, bacon, lemon juice and zest, with a good pinch of salt and pepper, continue to fry for another 3–5 minutes. Return the bacon to the pan, stir well and serve immediately.

LEMONY PUDDINGS

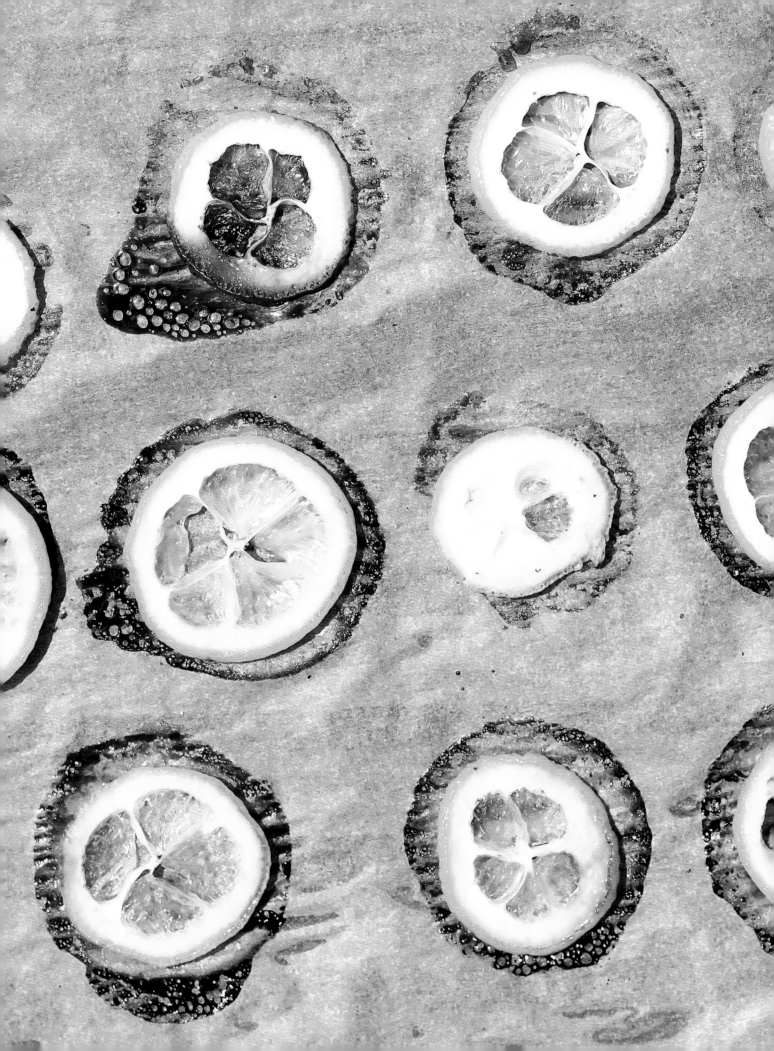

LIMONCELLO POLENTA CAKE

225g	caster sugar
250g	butter
3	lemons, juice & zest
3	eggs, separated
165g	ground almonds
160g	fine polenta
80ml	Limoncello

Preheat the oven to 170°C/325°F/Gas 3. Grease and flour a 20cm diameter cake tin. Combine the sugar, butter and zest in a bowl, using a hand-held blender, whisk together until smooth. Beat in the egg yolks, stir in juice, ground almonds and polenta. Clean the beaters and, in another bowl, whisk the egg whites into stiff peaks. Fold the whites into the polenta mixture, carefully blending. Transfer to the cake tin and bake for 50 minutes. Remove from the oven and drizzle the Limoncello evenly over the top. Unmould the cake and serve warm or cold.

SOUFFLÉ MILANESE

5	eggs, separated
450g	caster sugar
3	lemons, juice & zest
2 sachets	gelatine (14g), in 60ml boiling water
300ml	double cream
2	lemons, grated zest for decoration

Combine the yolks and sugar in a bain-marie. Over medium heat, whisk the mixture for 15 minutes, until it is thick. Stir in the lemon juice and zest and continue whisking until it coats the back of a spoon. Turn the heat off and put the container holding the mixture into a bowl of cold water. Continue whisking until the mixture has cooled completely. Add the gelatine and stir to combine.

In another bowl, whisk the cream until it is thick and fold it into the egg and lemon mixture. Put the container in the fridge and chill for 45 minutes. In another bowl, beat the egg whites until they form stiff peaks. Use a metal spoon to fold the whites into the chilled mixture. Transfer the combined mixture to a soufflé dish and pop into the fridge overnight. Decorate with lemon zest and serve.

CITRUS DELIGHT PUDDING

A healthy tasty treat, why is it healthy? Well as far as puddings go, Citrus Delight is a lighter option, without losing any scrummy taste. Honey, cinnamon and lemon are known to assist weight loss, plus no butter is used and there is less sugar, so get baking!

Serves 4

894g	**mandarin segments in juice, drained (3 × 298g tins)**
1 tbsp	**runny honey**
¼ tsp	**cinnamon**
½ tsp	**vanilla extract**
2	**lemons, juice ½ & zest 2**
1	**egg**
113g	**sugar**
100ml	**milk**
100ml	**sunflower oil**
180g	**flour**

Preheat the oven to 180°C/350°F/Gas 4. Take a square oven dish about 22·5cm × 7·5cm deep and line it with a mixture of mandarin slices, honey, cinnamon, vanilla and lemon juice.

Make the batter in a large bowl, combining the egg, sugar, milk, oil, flour and zest, stirring with a wooden spoon. When smooth, spoon the mixture over the mandarin segments distributing it evenly. Bake on the middle shelf of the oven for 30–35 minutes or until golden brown. Eat with a healthy conscience.

ZESTY EXOTIC MARBLED SURPRISE

I like to make batches of these at Christmas and experiment with the toppings, they make perfect gifts.

150g	**dark chocolate**
1 tsp	**caraway seeds**
2 tsp	**cocoa powder**
150g	**milk chocolate**
2	**lemons, zest only**
25g	**dried cranberries, chopped**

In a metal bowl, suspended over a saucepan of boiling water, without touching the water, combine and melt the dark chocolate, caraway seeds and cocoa powder. When the chocolate has completely melted, pour quickly onto a silicone sheet or parchment paper, tapping down lightly on a hard surface to flatten. Repeat process with a clean bowl, by melting the milk chocolate, pour over the dark chocolate, marble with a fork, sprinkle over the zest and cranberries, transfer to the fridge until set.

Keep in a slab if it is for a present, or if for a dinner party, I usually like to break it into chunks, serving in a pretty basket or on a silver platter.

ZESTY EXOTIC MARBLED SURPRISE

LEMON GLACÉ ICING

This mixture is sufficient to cover a 15–20cm cake.

240g	**icing sugar**
1	**large lemon, juice only**

Combine both sugar and juice in a saucepan over low heat, stir until dissolved. Although characteristically a smooth runnier icing, the mixture should be thick enough to coat the back of a spoon. Adjust consistency with more sugar or juice to thin or to thicken, spread lovingly over your cake for a glossy finish.

AMBELIA BREEZE

I wanted to include a gluten-free pudding. Whilst sitting with girlfriends in their home up in Ambelia (a gorgeous mountain spot found in North Cyprus) we came up with these flavours. Having taken it to a neighbours gathering later that day... Put it this way, none was left and I even had enquires for orders...

200g	**butter, softened**
200g	**light brown soft sugar**
4	**eggs**
175g	**whole almonds, broken in a mortar and pestle**
250g	**smooth mashed potato (roughly 2 skinned medium potatoes)**
2	**lemons, zest & juice**
1	**orange, 1 zest & ½ juice**
5cm	**cubed fresh ginger, peeled & grated**
1 tbsp	**gluten-free baking powder**
60g	**light brown soft sugar**

Preheat the oven to 180ºC/350°F/Gas 4. Grease a 20cm loose-bottomed cake tin. With an electric mixer, beat the butter and 200g sugar together until fluffy, adding the egg while beating. Fold in the almonds, cold mashed potato, lemon and orange zests, ginger and baking powder.

Pour the mixture into the tin, level the top and bake for 40–50 minutes or until golden. Leaving the pudding in its tin, transfer the tin to a wire rack. Make the drizzle by mixing 60g sugar, with the lemon juice and the juice of half an orange, spoon over the top of the pudding, letting it soak in. Cool completely before turning out and serving.

BANANA, CHOCOLATE & STRAWBERRY GOO
WITH A LEMON & PISTACHIO CRUMBLE

This invention came about whilst harking back to my childhood love of banana crumble (I loved experimenting even then, if you can have apple, why not banana!) I think all the flavours go marvelously together and others say so too, but don't take our word for it, try it yourself...

Serves 6

**Banana, Chocolate
& Strawberry Goo**

2	**lemons, juice & zest**
2	**large bananas, sliced**
150g	**dark chocolate, cubed**
500g	**fresh strawberries, thickly sliced**

Lemon & Pistachio Crumble

200g	**plain flour**
	Pinch salt
100g	**butter, cold, cubed**
90g	**shelled pistachios, broken**
100g	**demerara sugar**

Preheat the oven to 170°C/325°F/Gas 3. Zest the lemon into a dish and put aside. Place the banana slices, chocolate, strawberries and lemon juice into a large baking dish (9½ inch diameter × 3 inch deep) give it a good stir to combine.

To make the lemon & pistachio crumble, combine the flour, salt, and butter in a large bowl, rub together with your finger tips until the mixture resembles course breadcrumbs. Stir in the pistachios, sugar and zest, mix again. Sprinkle the crumble evenly over the fruit and chocolate and bake in the oven until golden, about an hour. Serve warm or cold.

THREE ZEST MACADAMIA SHORTBREAD

This came about when experimenting with the tasty marriage of the three citrus fruits, I think it works rather well...

225g	**plain flour**
100g	**corn flour**
100g	**icing sugar**
225g	**butter, cubed**
60g	**macadamia nuts, broken**
1	**large lemon, zest only**
1	**large lime, zest only**
1	**large orange, zest only**
½ tsp	**vanilla extract**

Preheat the oven to 180°C/350°F/Gas 4. In a large bowl, put all the ingredients in and mix together with your hands, until combined well. Press into a swiss roll tin, making sure it is an even thickness all over, use the back of a spoon if necessary to even it out. Prick in a nice linear pattern all over with a fork. Cook for 30 minutes.

Remove from the oven and cut into rectangles but leave the shortbread in the tin to cool (cooling will be helped by placing the tin on a wire rack). Once cooled, serve.

SWEET LEMON BUTTER

I love to serve this up to guests on toast the morning after a sleepover.

125g	**butter**
3	**lemons, juice & zest**
225g	**caster sugar**
2	**eggs**

Combine butter, lemon juice and sugar in a pan on a high heat until dissolved, stirring for 5 minutes. In a bowl, beat the eggs well. Tip the hot syrup over the eggs, continuously stirring. Return to heat and cook, stirring continuously, for another 5 minutes.

Remove from heat, add lemon zest, stir... Done. Store in sterilised sealed jars. Refrigerate after opening and enjoy!

ROSE SCENTED LEMON MERINGUE PIE

I wanted to make a lemon meringue pie with a difference, this delicate tasting pie is fit for a Princess...

220g	**white sugar**
3 tbsp	**cornflour**
2	**lemon, 2 zest, 1 juice**
1 tsp	**rose extract**
3	**eggs, separated**
360ml	**boiling water**
1	**baked pie shell***
80g	**caster sugar**

Preheat the oven to 220°C/425°F/Gas 7. Mix the white sugar with the cornflour. Stir in the zest, lemon juice and rose extract. Separate the eggs, beat the egg yolks, mix them into the sugar lemon mixture and combine well. Gradually stir in the boiling water. Continue to cook on medium heat, stirring occasionally. Continue to boil the rose custard for 5 minutes, stirring constantly.

Transfer the rose custard into the baked pie shell and allow to cool. Beat egg whites until they begin to form soft peaks. Gradually add the caster sugar while continuing to beat until the mixture forms stiff peaks. Spread the egg whites over the cooled rose custard, covering evenly. Bake for 10–15 minutes until the meringue is golden-brown. Once cool, serve.

*18cm diameter × 2cm deep. You could also make your own shortcrust pastry, lining a pie dish.

SWEET LEMON BUTTER, SHOWN WITH RUSSIAN LEMON SUGAR

BLUEBERRY & LEMON RICOTTA CAKE

BLUEBERRY & LEMON RICOTTA CAKE

Gluten-free

250g	ricotta cheese
140g	soft butter
140g	ground almonds
140g	golden caster sugar
6	medium eggs, separated
1	lemon, zest & juice
75g	dried blueberries
25g	fine polenta flour
	Icing sugar, for dusting

Preheat the oven to 180°C/350°F/Gas 4. Grease and line the base of a 23cm diameter springform tin. Put the ricotta, butter, almonds, sugar and egg yolks in a large bowl and beat with a wooden spoon until creamy. Add the lemon zest and juice with the dried blueberries.

Whisk the egg whites in a clean bowl until they form soft peaks. Fold the polenta into the ricotta mixture, then gently fold in the whisked egg whites. Pour the cake mix into the prepared tin and bake for 35 minutes. The cake is cooked when it is golden and just firm to the touch. Allow it to cool in the tin, then transfer to a serving plate and dust with the icing sugar before serving.

LEMON CHEESECAKE WITH A POMEGRANATE SAUCE

As a lover of pomegranates (universal symbol of luck & fertility) I wanted to create a cake using them...

Base

12	plain digestive biscuits
50g	butter
1 tsp	lemon extract

Cheesecake Filling

2 tbsp	clear honey
500g	ricotta cheese
3	eggs
175g	caster sugar
1 tsp	lemon extract
200g	crème fraîche
2	lemons, zest only

Pomegranate Sauce

3 tsp	arrow root
280g	pomegranate seeds
100g	caster sugar
1	lemon, juice only

Preheat the oven to 180°C/350°F/Gas 4. Crush the biscuits, mix well with the butter and lemon extract and press into a 20cm diameter cake tin with a removable bottom. Put all the cheesecake filling ingredients into a blender, blend until smooth. Pour on top of the biscuit base, tap gently on a firm surface to level. Bake for 50–60 minutes, remove and leave to cool completely. When cool, put into the fridge overnight.

Remove the cheesecake from the tin, transfer on to a serving plate. Make the pomegranate sauce by firstly mixing the arrow root with a little water in a small bowl, add this to the pomegranate seeds, sugar, and lemon juice in a pan. Heat whilst continuously stirring until the mixture resembles a syrup. You could let the sauce cool or serve warm over the cold cheesecake. Don't worry that it will drip down the sides, adds to the charm.

LEMON SORBET IN LEMON SHELLS

8	**large lemons**
340g	**sugar**
360ml	**water**
6	**lemons, zest only**

Cut off the top ⅓ of the lemons, opposite the stem end and reserve for the 'cap.' Hollow out each lemon, then discard the pips and pith and put the juice and flesh into a blender. Slice a little off the bottom of each lemon shell, being careful not to cut through to the inside of the lemon. This will make them sit straight when placed on a plate.

Freeze the shells at least 1 hour or overnight. Then fill with sorbet (made as per instructions below) and freeze again.

To make the sorbet, combine the sugar, blended lemon juice and flesh and water in a saucepan, over a medium heat, stir until the sugar has dissolved. Remove from the heat. Grate the zest from the other 6 lemons and add to the lemon/sugar mixture, stir. Set aside and allow to cool.

Methods

Ice Cream Maker – transfer the mixture to an ice cream maker and freeze according to manufacturer's instructions.

Freezer Method – pour into a container, cover and place the mixture in the freezer. When it is semi-solid, break it up with a fork and freeze again.

Fill each frozen lemon shell with the sorbet, top with a lemon cap, then freeze again until completely frozen, before serving.

This delicious pudding can be prepared 2–3 days in advance, simply keep covered in a container stored in the freezer.

GRUYÈRE & CRANBERRY TART

Out of all the cheeses Gruyère is possibly the most renowned for being an ideal pairing to lemon, I like the taste of cheese with cranberries, therefore this Gruyère tart came about...

Serves 10

Crust

170g	flour
	Pinch salt
85g	butter
105g	caster sugar
40ml	milk

Gruyère & Cranberry Filling

	Dried cranberries
1	egg, beaten
300g	natural yogurt
25g	sugar
1	lemon, juice & zest
190g	Gruyère, grated

Preheat the oven to 200°C/400°F/Gas 6. Sift the flour and salt into a bowl and rub in the butter with the tips of your fingers until the consistency is that of breadcrumbs. Stir in the sugar and milk and keep stirring to create a dough. Roll out the dough to line a 22·5cm diameter x 3cm deep tin. There may be some dough left over. For the filling, combine the remaining ingredients in a bowl, mix well and transfer to the lined tart tin. Bake for 40–50 minutes. Allow to cool before cutting into slices and serving.

APRICOT & ALMOND TART

Serves 10

Crust

245g	plain flour
2	small lemons, zest only
95g	icing sugar
	Pinch salt
1 tsp	almond essence
230g	butter

Almond Filling

45g	blanched almonds
100g	dried apricots
60g	ground almonds
80g	sugar
3	eggs
120ml	single cream
1 tsp	almond essence

Preheat the oven to 180°C/350°F/Gas 4. In a bowl, combine the flour, zest, icing sugar, salt, almond essence and butter and gently knead the mixture into a ball. Press into the base of a greased 22·5cm diameter × 3cm deep tin, make a few rows of holes with a fork. Bake for around 15 minutes. Place aside to cool slightly, leaving the oven on.

Prepare the Almond Filling by mixing the rest of the ingredients in a blender, blitz until well combined. Transfer into your crust and bake for half an hour or until the edges brown. Tasty served both warm or cold, I like it warm with some thick plain yogurt.

MUM'S LEMON CARROT CAKE

A 'lemonised' version of one of my fav cakes, do try it, although no-one makes it quite like Mum!

160g	**plain flour**
210g	**sugar**
1 tsp	**baking powder**
1 tsp	**allspice**
1 tsp	**cinnamon**
1 tsp	**nutmeg**
½ tsp	**baking soda**
½ tsp	**salt**
3	**eggs, separated**
190g	**grated carrots**
2	**lemons, finely grated zest**
200ml	**Mazola or sunflower oil**

Cream Cheese Icing

225g	**Philadelphia cheese**
80g	**butter, softened**
2	**lemons, finely grated zest**
350g	**Icing sugar**

Preheat the oven to 180°C/350°F/Gas 4. Sift all the dry ingredients into a large bowl. Separate the eggs, add the yolks, carrots, lemon zest and oil into the dry mix and stir well until thoroughly incorporated. Now beat the egg whites and fold into the mixture carefully, with a metal spoon until completely mixed in. Transfer to a greased and floured, loose-bottomed 20cm × 9cm deep cake tin. Tap it gently on a flat surface to settle the contents.

Bake for about 50 minutes on the middle shelf of the oven. It is done when it springs back when touched. Carefully turn out onto a wire rack, and leave to cool completely. To make the icing, mix together the Philadelphia, butter and lemon zest, then beat in the icing sugar. Spread generously all over cooled cake. Scrumptious.

BRIOCHE BREAD PUDDING
WITH LEMON & EARL GREY TEA SAUCE

The lemony answer to comfort food... Born out of my affection for Earl Grey Tea.

2	**eggs, slightly beaten**
450ml	**milk**
1 tsp	**vanilla**
½ tsp	**cinnamon**
200g	**brioche, cubed**
100g	**brown sugar**
90g	**sultanas**

Earl Grey Tea Sauce

1 tbsp	**cornflour**
100g	**sugar**
250ml	**boiling water, (infused briefly with 1 tea bag Earl Grey)**
1	**lemon, juice & zest**
⅛ tsp	**nutmeg**
	Pinch salt
1 tbsp	**butter**

Preheat the oven to 180°C/350°F/Gas 4. In a bowl lightly combine all of the pudding ingredients, being careful not to break up the brioche too much. Pour into a 25 × 12 × 7·5cm rectangular ovenware dish. Bake for 45 minutes or until a knife inserted in the centre comes out clean.

Now for the all-important sauce. Mix together the cornflour, sugar and boiling water and bring to the boil. Whisk over a low heat until the liquid becomes syrupy. Stir in the lemon juice & zest, nutmeg, salt and butter.

When the pudding is ready, spoon half the sauce over it, reserving the rest in a jug for guests to add more if desired. This pudding is tasty both hot and cold.

LIMONCELLO MOUSSE

I dreamt this up on my return from a mesmorising research trip to Campania. Using Limoncello kindly given to me by Mariano Valentino Vinaccia, founder of the Solagri co-operative, which exists to promote and protect the Sorrentine lemon. He says "when you take a lemon, it is but a yellow fruit, Sorrento lemon, is a lemon!" I can see his point... They certainly are particularly special...

Serves 4

284ml	**double cream**
1	**lemon, zest & juice**
60g	**caster sugar**
50ml	**Limoncello**
2	**eggs, whites only**
2	**lemons, zest only for garnish**

In a large bowl combine the cream, zest and sugar, whisk until fairly thick, add in the lemon juice and Limoncello, whisk a little more. In a separate bowl whisk the egg whites, when soft peaks form, fold into the lemon mixture. Spoon the mouse into four serving bowls and refrigerate, once they have all set, sprinkle lemon zest over the top, serve.

BRIOCHE BREAD PUDDING WITH LEMON & EARL GREY TEA SAUCE

BERGAMOT & HONEY ICE CREAM

A yummy perfumed sweet delight. After receiving a deliciously fragrant fresh bergamot in the post all the way from Bodrum; Turkey, a few hours later this inspiration came to fruition.

1½ tbsp	**bergamot zest**
2 tbsp	**runny honey**
190g	**soft brown sugar**
250ml	**milk**
1 tsp	**vanilla extract**
245ml	**double cream**
35ml	**bergamot juice**

In a blender combine the bergamot zest, honey, sugar and milk, blend until well combined, next stir in the vanilla extract. In a separate bowl, with an electric whisk, whip the cream and bergamot juice until stiff. Combine both mixtures and again using your electric whisk, blend together until smooth and well incorporated. Pour the mixture into a freezable container and cover with cling film. Freeze for 3 hours, or until firm. Serve!

CANDIED CITRON & LEMON COOKIES

My buttery, crumbley cookies with a zing are always a firm favourite, a well received treat when visiting friends.

Makes 24

115g	**butter**
35g	**caster sugar**
2	**egg yolks**
1 tsp	**vanilla extract**
30g	**candied lemon peel, thinly sliced**
30g	**candied citron peel, thinly sliced**
125g	**plain flour**
40g	**corn flour**
1½ tsp	**baking powder**
	Pinch salt

Using an electric mixer beat the butter and sugar together until smooth. Mix in egg yolks, vanilla, lemon and citron peels.

Next combine the flours, baking powder and salt in a bowl. Add in the butter mixture, mix until it just begins to combine. Shape into two even logs. Cover tightly in greaseproof paper, and put into the fridge for 2 hours.

Preheat the oven to 170°C/325°F/Gas 3. Line a baking sheet with greaseproof paper. Slice the logs into 1cm thick rounds and bake for 15 minutes, or until golden. Transfer to wire racks, allowing to cool before distributing with love.

CANDIED CITRON & LEMON COOKIES

LEMON & JUNIPER BERRY SEED CAKE

LEMON & JUNIPER BERRY SEED CAKE

Knowing juniper berries and lemon are a great match, I thought, why not in a cake?

280g	plain flour
2 tsp	baking powder
	Pinch salt
115g	butter
200g	caster sugar
2	large eggs
2 tsp	ground coriander
2	lemons, zest only
1 tsp	mace
180ml	milk
100g	currants
2 tsp	caraway seeds
1½ tsp	dried juniper berries, crushed

Preheat the oven to 180°C/350°F/Gas 4. Grease and flour a 24 × 7cm loaf tin. Sift together flour, baking powder, and salt into a bowl. In a separate bowl, using an electric mixer, cream the butter and sugar until fluffy. Add the eggs, coriander, lemon zest and mace and mix well. On a low speed add the flour mixture, alternating with milk. Stir in the currants, caraway seeds and juniper berries, again mixing well.

Pour the batter into the tin, tapping on a work surface to level the contents. Place on the middle shelf of the oven and bake for 1 hour, until a knife inserted in the centre comes out clean. Cool on a wire rack for 10 minutes, before turning out to finish cooling. If desired decorate with candied lemon slices. Delicious served with lemon butter (p.118).

VEGAN BRAZIL NUT, CARDAMOM & LEMON BISCOTTI

Biscotti recipes hark all the way back to the 13th century in Italy. I devised these twice-cooked biscuits ('bis' meaning twice and 'cotti' cooked, in Italian) because I wanted something vegan in my book, having been vegan for a little while, then vegetarian, now eating virtually everthing... Hope you will agree even a carnivore would happily munch their way through them.

180g	silken tofu
190g	caster sugar
80ml	olive oil
2	lemons, 2 zest, 1½ juice
1 tsp	vanilla essence
8	cardamom pods, seeds only, pounded in a pestle & mortar
60g	broken brazil nuts
375g	plain flour
170g	semolina flour
1 tsp	bicarbonate of soda
1 tsp	baking powder
	Pinch salt

Preheat the oven to 190°C/375°F/Gas 5. In a blender, put the tofu, sugar, oil, lemon zest and juice, vanilla and pounded cardamom seeds. In a bowl, mix together the nuts, flours, bicarbonate of soda, baking powder and salt, stir in the tofu mixture.

On an oiled baking sheet, split dough into 2 even 22·5cm logs. Bake for 30 minutes. Remove from oven, leaving to cool for 20 minutes. Reduce the oven temperature to 150°F/300°F/Gas 2. Slice the logs into roughly 1cm deep rounds and lay them on a parchment paper lined baking sheet. Bake for 70 minutes, turning once half way through. When cool, serve with a smile and a hot drink to dunk them into.

GLOBAL LEMONY GRUB

Albanian	limon
Arabic	شجرة الليمون
Breton	sitron
Catalan	llimona
Chinese	檸檬
Croatian	limun
Czech	citrón; citrónový
Danish	citron
Dutch	citroen
Esperanto	citrono
Estonian	sidrun
Finnish	sitruuna
French	citron
Georgian	ლიმონი
German	zitrone
Greek	λεμόνιο
Hungarian	pezsgőpor
Icelandic	sítróna
Indonesian	jeruk lemon
Italia	limone
Japanese	レモン
Latvian	citrons
Lithuanian	citrine
Norwegian	sitron
Polish	cytryna
Portugese	limão
Romanian	lămâie
Russian	лимон
Slovak	citron
Slovinian	limona
Spanish	limon
Swedish	citron
Turkish	limon
Vietnamese	quả chanh
Walloon	citron

AFGHANISTAN

CHATNI SAUCE

Chatni is the traditional Afghani condiment, offered with every meal. Perhaps vinegar is more commonly used, but, as I am sure you would concur, lemon adds a certain 'je ne sais quoi' and is often substituted as a preference...

2	**lemons, juice only**
60ml	**olive oil**
30ml	**water**
50g	**walnuts**
4	**cloves garlic**
1 tsp	**sugar**
1 tsp	**salt**
1–2	**green chillis, deseeded**
2	**handfuls fresh coriander**
	Handful fresh mint

In a blender, combine all the ingredients together until smooth and serve.

AKROTIRI

LEMON MARINADE FOR MEAT

Lemon features heavily in local marinades, commonly used with pork and lamb. Leaving to marinade overnight is best. The marinade is also suitable for chicken and seafood, in which case a couple of hours marinating is sufficient.

45ml	**olive oil**
2	**lemons, juice only**
3	**cloves garlic, crushed**
1 tsp	**dry oregano leaves**
	Pinch salt & pepper

Whisk together the oil and lemon juice. Add the garlic, oregano, salt and pepper and stir to combine. Ensure the meat is steeped entirely in the marinade, covered well and refrigerated. When marinated, cook as desired.

ALBANIA

HONEY & WALNUT CAKE

Albanians sure like their walnuts and honey, as do I. Every morning (well most) starts off with porridge and a decent spoonful of organic honey, always, if possible, from a friend's beehive. Followed by a sprinkle of walnuts. Hence, my easy motivation for this sweet Albanian inspired cake...

Cake

110g	sugar
1 tsp	orange extract
3 tbsp	organic lavender honey
100g	butter
2	eggs
230g	plain flour
1 tsp	baking powder
1 tsp	bicarbonate of soda
½ tsp	cinnamon
180g	plain organic yogurt
1	lemon, zest (juice needed for glaze)
1	orange, zest only
100g	walnut pieces, toasted

Glaze

80ml	water
90g	sugar
½ tsp	cinnamon
1	lemon, juice only
¼ tsp	ground allspice
¼ tsp	ground cloves

Preheat the oven to 180°C/350°F/Gas 4. In a large mixing bowl, combine the sugar, orange extract, honey and butter. Beat with an electric whisk, add in the eggs and continue beating. Next add the flour, baking powder, bicarbonate of soda, cinnamon and yogurt, whisking until smooth. Stir the zests and walnuts into the mix. Transfer the batter to a greased and floured 23 × 33cm cake tin and bake for an hour or until an inserted knife comes out clean.

To make the glaze, simmer all the ingredients over a medium heat in a saucepan, stirring until the sugar dissolves. Pour over the hot cake. Return to the oven for another 8 minutes. Can be served warm or allowed to cool.

ALGERIA

CHTIT'HA DJEDJ (CHICKEN & CHICKPEA STEW)

A delicious and warming hearty family meal, with a distinctive North African flavour, straight from Algeria.

Serve 4–6

60ml	**olive oil**
1 tsp	**ras al hanout**
1 tsp	**harissa**
¼ tsp	**ginger powder**
	Pinch salt
2	**cloves garlic, crushed**
500g	**chicken breast, cubed**
1	**handful coriander, chopped**
1	**handful parsley, chopped**
1	**stick cinnamon**
1	**small red onion, chopped**
400g	**can chickpeas (drained)**
1	**lemon, juice only**

In a bowl, with a spoon, mix together 30ml olive oil, ras al hanout, harissa, ginger, salt and garlic. Now throw in the chicken to the mix, stir to coat the cubes evenly. Cover and leave in the fridge to marinate overnight. The next day, in a saucepan, place the marinated chicken with half the coriander and parsley, cinnamon stick and enough water to just cover it. Bring to boil, reduce the heat and simmer for 50 minutes. With a slotted spoon, remove the cooked chicken from the saucepan, reserving the liquid inside.

In a frying pan, heat 30ml olive oil, caramelise the onions until golden, add to the chicken liquid in the saucepan, along with the chickpeas. Bring to the boil, reduce the heat and simmer until it has the consistency of a watery sauce. Add the lemon juice, stir and take off the heat. Discard the cinnamon stick, then return the chicken to the saucepan. Give it a stir, sprinkle with the remaining parsley and coriander and serve.

AMERICA

BUTTERNUT SQUASH PIE WITH MARSHMALLOW TOPPING

Pastry

300g	**plain flour**
2	**lemons, zest only**
40g	**icing sugar**
165g	**butter**
2	**egg yolks, beaten**

Filling

1·7kg	**butternut squash**
30ml	**water**
200g	**maple syrup**
1½ tsp	**cinnamon**
1½ tsp	**ground ginger**
¼ tsp	**ground cloves**
½ tsp	**nutmeg**
3	**eggs, beaten**
200ml	**evaporated milk**

Garnish

140g	**mini white marshmallows**

Put flour, zest, icing sugar and butter in a bowl. Chop up the butter with a knife, lightly rubbing between your fingertips, until the mixture has the texture of breadcrumbs. Add egg yolk, mix and form a ball, cover with cling film, pop into the fridge for 30 minutes. Preheat the oven to 200°C/400°F/Gas 6. Halve the squash, scoop out seeds and fibres, quarter, drizzle the water over the top and cook skin-side up in a roasting tin for 30 minutes.

Grease and flour a 30cm diameter tart tin with a removable bottom. Roll out the dough to fit the tin. Prick all over with a fork. Cover the dough with parchment paper and fill with baking beans. Bake for 15 minutes, then remove the paper and beans and bake for another 5 minutes or until golden.

Remove the squash from the oven, allow to cool and peel off the skin. Using a hand-blender, purée the squash flesh. Push it through a fine sieve lined with muslin, suspended over a bowl and leave to drain for an hour.

Discard the liquid and transfer 500g of purée to a bowl. Stir in the maple syrup, spices, eggs and evaporated milk, until well combined. Pour the mixture into the pastry case and bake for 20 minutes. Dot with the marshmallows and bake for a further 20 minutes. Allow to cool on a wire rack for at least an hour before serving.

ANDORRA

ESCUDELLA (HEARTY SOUP)

Escudella Day is celebrated in all parishes on Saint Anthony's Day, January 17ᵗʰ...

Serves 4

6	**sausages, best quality**
1 tbsp	**olive oil**
380g	**chicken breast, cubed**
2	**bacon rashers, pieces**
1	**potato (380g), 5cm cubes**
1	**tin cannellini beans, rinsed & drained**
	Salt & white pepper, to taste
120g	**leek, sliced**
60g	**dry pasta shells**
25g	**rice**
300g	**chicken stock**
½	**lemon, pips discarded**

Skin the sausages, make 3 balls of sausage meat per sausage, leaving you with 18 balls. Heat the olive oil in a large saucepan, fry the sausage balls, chicken and bacon until slightly golden, around 5 minutes. Add the remaining ingredients, with enough water to cover, bring to a boil, cover and simmer for half an hour. Serve.

ANGOLA

MUAMBA DE GALINHA (CHICKEN STEW)

Deriving a unique taste from the all important palm oil, I find this extremely satisfying, simply served alone, a big comforting bowl of this stew should make your tummy smile... yum.

Serves 4

2	**lemons, juice only**
3	**cloves garlic**
2	**pinches salt**
1	**small green fresh chilli (2 if you like it hotter)**
400g	**chicken breast, cubed**
120g	**red palm oil**
3	**small onions, diced**
3	**plum tomatoes, diced**
420g	**butternut squash, 2cm cubes**
180g	**whole okra**
320ml	**water**

Using a blender, combine the lemon juice, garlic, 1 pinch salt and chilli, blitz until smooth, this is the marinade for the chicken. Marinate the chicken for 1 hour minimum, after stirring around with a spoon, ensuring the pieces are well coated. When the chicken has marinated, drain but reserve the liquid in a bowl.

In a large saucepan, heat the palm oil until piping hot, add the chicken pieces, fry until just lightly golden. Remove with a slotted spoon. Replace with the onions and fry until translucent. Next add the remaining ingredients to the saucepan, including the marinated chicken. Simmer on low heat for 30 minutes or until tender.

ANGUILLA

GRILLED LOBSTER WITH LEMON HERB BUTTER

1	**whole lobster**
	Salt & pepper, to taste
450g	**butter**
1	**fresh clove garlic, chopped**
1 tbsp	**lemon juice**
1 tsp	**fresh spring onion, chopped**

Cut the lobster in half, season with salt and pepper. Grill for 5 minutes, then place in the oven for 8 minutes at 180°C/350°F/Gas 4. Heat the butter in a small saucepan, add in the chopped garlic and lemon juice. Finally, add in the chopped spring onion, give it a stir and pour over the grilled lobster halves. A way to taste the Caribbean, even if you are cooking it in colder climes.

ANTIGUA AND BARBUDA
PORK CHOPS WITH BACON WRAPPED BLACK PINEAPPLE

Home to the famous black pineapple, whose name derives from its almost black exterior signalling it is fully ripe, I could not do a recipe for Antigua & Barbuda without it. The significance of the pineapple translates not only in their local food, both savoury and sweet, but also can be found as a motif intertwined in their traditional art and furniture carvings. Serve with mashed cassava or sweet potato, or anything that will soak up the tasty juices.

Serves 2

1	**lemon, 1 zest & ½ juice**
40g	**butter, softened**
	Pinch salt & pepper
½ tbsp	**cumin**
2	**pork chops, fat removed**
3	**rashers smoked bacon**
20g	**brown sugar**
6	**black pineapple,* 2·5cm cubes**

Preheat the oven to 220°C/425°F/Gas 7. Blend together the lemon juice and zest, butter, salt, pepper and cumin. Rub the paste over both sides of your chops. Halve each bacon rasher, drench the 6 pieces in the brown sugar and wrap a piece around each pineapple chunk, securing with a toothpick. Put the chops in a baking tray with the bacon wrapped chunks scattered around. Bake for 15 minutes, turn the chops and chunks over and cook for another 15 minutes. They are ready to serve.

*If black pineapple is unattainable, any pineapple would be as good!

ARGENTINA
CHIMICHURRI (SAUCE)

Any Argentinian steak feels naked without this divine sauce... Likewise, it goes beautifully well with most meats.

120ml	**olive oil**
1	**lemon, juice only**
	Small handful fresh parsley, finely chopped
2	**cloves garlic, crushed**
2 tbsp	**red wine vinegar**
½ tsp	**basil**
½ tsp	**dried oregano**
1	**green chilli, deseeded**
	Pinch salt & pepper

In a blender, combine all the ingredients and blitz until completely amalgamated.

ARMENIA

WALNUT & YOGURT CAKE SOAKED IN LEMON-MINT SYRUP

I have to say, I am a huge fan of cakes which involve yogurt, they have a sharp/sweet flavour and a density to them which I love. The stars of this cake are walnuts and mint; both Armenian staples, enjoy...

200g	**butter**
140g	**sugar**
220g	**organic plain yogurt**
2	**large eggs**
½	**lemon, juice only**
240g	**plain flour**
½ tsp	**bicarbonate of soda**
40g	**walnut pieces**

Lemon-Mint Syrup

180g	**sugar**
1	**lemon, juice & zest**
180ml	**water**
3	**sprigs fresh mint**

Preheat the oven to 180°C/350°F/Gas 4. Grease and flour a circular cake tin with removable bottom 20cm in diameter × 5cm deep. Using an electric mixer, in a large bowl, beat the butter and sugar until light and fluffy. Tip in the yogurt, eggs and lemon juice and mix well. Sift in the flour plus bicarbonate of soda, add the walnuts, again mixing well. Pour the batter into the tin, transfer to the oven and bake until golden, around 40 minutes. Remove, leaving in the tin, put aside to cool.

Now make the syrup by putting all the ingredients into a saucepan. Bring to the boil over a medium heat. Stir until the sugar has completely dissolved. Remove from the heat, discard the mint sprigs and pour gradually and evenly over the cake until entirely absorbed. Serve!

ARUBA

ARUBA COCKTAIL

The Orgeat syrup shines through, in essence it is an almond syrup, deriving from the Italian word 'orzata', meaning almond. Lemon and almond complement each other beautifully...

Serves 1

60ml	**gin**
15ml	**white curacao**
½	**egg white, whipped**
1	**lemon, juice only**
1 tsp	**Orgeat syrup**
4	**ice cubes**

Combine the ingredients in a cocktail shaker, shake, strain into a cocktail glass and serve.

AUSTRALIA
LEMONGRASS LAMINGTONS

Lamingtons are named after the Governor of Queensland from 1896–1901, Charles Wallace Alexander Napier Cochrane-Baillie, second Baron Lamington. The lamington is indisputably the national cake. Lemongrass, native to Australia, with its unique fantastical aroma, can be bought in most supermarkets. That said, chefs advise using lemon zest in a recipe as a substitute, if you cannot find any...

Makes 12

Cake
4	eggs, separated
120g	sugar
1 tsp	vanilla extract
75g	self-raising flour
40g	plain flour
30g	cornflour

Lemongrass Icing
210g	butter, softened
210g	icing sugar, sifted
½	small lemon, juice
1	stalk lemongrass, liquidated with 50ml water

Garnish
100g	desiccated coconut

Preheat the oven to 180°C/350°F/Gas 4. Line a 20cm × 20cm × 3cm tin with greaseproof paper. In a large bowl, beat the egg whites until soft peaks form, add the sugar, continuing beating. Add in the egg yolks and vanilla. Using a large metal spoon, fold in the flours carefully. Transfer the mixture into the tin, bake for half an hour or until the cake is springy to the touch. Leave for a few minutes before turning out onto a wire rack to cool.

When cool, cut into 12 squares. Make the icing by combining all the ingredients with an electric whisk, beat together until well combined and smooth. Spread onto the cake squares, covering every side and then dip into the coconut.

AUSTRIA

KAISERSCHMARRN WITH CLOVE & PLUM COMPOTE

This scrummy exorbitant breakfast is said to have been born in Vienna during the reign of Kaiser Franz Josef I (1848–1916). Legend has it that the Emperor relished eating pancakes for his pudding, but when they were not perfect and pleasing to the eye, he donated them to his servants, thus being nicknamed 'the Emperors' mess'. Traditionally, Kaiserschmarrn is served with Zwetschkenröster, a fruit compote made from Plums, which inspired my recipe...

Clove & Plum Compote

6	**pitted plums, sliced**
40g	**sugar**
½ tsp	**vanilla extract**
½ tsp	**ground cloves**
½	**lemon, juice only**

Pancake

3	**eggs, separated**
170g	**plain flour**
240ml	**milk**
40g	**sugar**
90g	**butter, melted**
30g	**sultanas**
½ tsp	**vanilla extract**
1	**lemon, zest only**
	Icing sugar, for dusting

Begin by making the compote. Combine all the ingredients, in a saucepan, bring to the boil, stirring, then reduce to a simmer, cooking until it is thick and with a compote texture, about 10 minutes.

In a mixing bowl, using an electric hand-whisk, beat the egg whites until they form soft peaks, then set aside. In another bowl, again using the hand-whisk, mix together the flour, milk, egg yolks, sugar, 70g butter, sultanas, vanilla and zest, ensure they are incorporated well. Gradually fold in the egg whites.

Melt 20g butter in a large frying pan to coat the bottom. When bubbling, pour in a 2·5cm layer of the pancake mix. Fry until golden, turn over once to cook the other side, again, until golden. When cooked, transfer to a serving dish and with 2 forks shred the pancake into strips. Dust with icing sugar and serve hot with the clove & plum compote.

AZERBAIJAN

LEMON & ROSE SHAKARBURA

Shakarbura are sweet turnovers that are eaten to celebrate Novruz Bayramı (The New Year holiday) a national holiday to signify both New Year and the coming of Spring. Preparations for Novruz begin a month prior, from extensive spring cleaning of the house, buying an abundance of candles for decoration, getting every family member a new outfit, painting eggs, flower arranging and of course preparing the edible treats, such as Shakarbura. Every Tuesday throughout that month is devoted to commemorating each of the elements; earth, water, fire and wind. The last Tuesday is devoted to wind, whereby people jump over bonfires, chanting phrases, hoping for any ill health they might have to pass and in turn to receive strength.

80ml	**organic semi-skimmed milk**
7g	**yeast**
	Pinch salt
½ tsp	**cardamom powder**
1	**egg**
240g	**plain flour**
60g	**butter, melted**

Lemon & Rose Filling

140g	**flaked almonds**
190g	**sugar**
40g	**desiccated coconut**
3	**lemons, zest only**
1 tsp	**rose extract**

Begin by warming the milk in a saucepan. In a mixing bowl, combine and knead together the yeast, salt, cardamom powder, egg, flour and butter. Cover the dough in the bowl with a tea-towel and leave it in a warm place for 1 hour.

After 50 minutes, preheat the oven to 180°C/350°F/Gas 4. Make the lemon and rose filling. Simply combine all the filling ingredients together in a blender, or grind them in a mortar with a pestle. Divide the dough into around 20 balls. Roll each ball out into a circle 2mm thick. Divide the filling evenly amongst all 20 circles. Seal the edges by pinching them together so they form a turnover shape. Bake for 30 minutes or until golden.

BAHAMAS
SWEET & SOUR CITRUS SALAD

Certainly an interesting salad with a delightful crunch, pleasantly complements most white fish, perfect accompanied by a large ice-cold glass of 'switcha', the local lemonade.

Dressing

1 tsp	sugar
2 tbsp	runny honey
3 tbsp	white wine vinegar
2 tbsp	poppy seeds
2	spring onions, finely sliced
½	lemon, juice & zest
	Pinch salt
1 tsp	wholegrain mustard

Salad

½	red bell pepper, thinly sliced
1	small red onion, thinly sliced
130g	guava slices, tinned is fine
160g	fresh pineapple chunks
½	red grapefruit, peeled & sliced
½	iceburg lettuce, shredded
4	meaty mushrooms, finely sliced

In a blender, combine the dressing ingredients, until well mixed. Toss together the salad ingredients in a large salad bowl, pour the dressing over the mixture, toss again and serve.

BANGLADESH

LEMON INFUSED DAAL

Best served with steamed plain basmati rice, or if you prefer bread, you could serve with a paratha. I am a fan of the taste of the typical Bangladeshi spice mix, known as punch pooran, literally translating as 'five spices', so could not resist dreaming up this recipe, for you to enjoy.

Serves 2

190g	**red split lentils**
2cm	**fresh ginger, peeled & chopped**
2	**red chillis, deseeded & sliced finely**
2	**cloves garlic, crushed**
½ tsp	**turmeric**
45ml	**water**
6	**lemon leaves**
70g	**ghee**
1	**red onion, finely chopped**
1 tsp	**punch pooran mix**
90g	**paneer, cubes**
½	**lemon, juice only**

Rinse the lentils in a fine-meshed sieve, under cold running water. Transfer to a saucepan and bring them to a boil with the ginger, chillies, garlic, turmeric and water. Reduce the heat, simmer until tender. When cooked, remove from the heat and use a hand-held electric blender to process until smooth. Return to the heat and add the lemon leaves. Bring to the boil, reduce the heat and cook for 10 minutes.

In a frying pan, heat the ghee and add the onions and punch pooran and cook until golden. Put the lentils into a serving bowl and sprinkle over the onions, paneer and lemon juice.

BARBADOS

PEPPERPOT (OXTAIL STEW)

Personally, I love the taste of oxtail when it is falling off the bone in a yummy stew, there is something really homely about it, I also enjoy HOT food, so this is a winner. Bear in mind that this stew is called pepperpot for a reason. If you would prefer it milder, only use half to one scotch bonnet. Serve as it is with a chunk of bread (Caribbean salt bread if you can find it) or rice, or indeed potato - enjoy my take on this classic Bajan meal.

Serves 2–4

455g	**diced lamb, on the bone**
1kg	**oxtail**
2	**lemons, juice only**
1 tbsp	**table salt**
½ tbsp	**brown sugar**
½	**large onion, sliced**
1	**large spring onion, sliced**
2	**cloves garlic, chopped**
2	**scotch bonnet peppers, cut in half**
1	**beef stock cube**
4	**whole bay leaves**
½ tsp	**cinnamon**
½ tsp	**dried thyme**
¼ tsp	**ground cloves**
¼ tsp	**dried oregano**
¼ tsp	**paprika**
	Pinch salt

Wash the lamb and oxtail in water. Drain, put into a bowl with the juice of 1 lemon and a tablespoon of salt, mix and leave for 30 minutes; a Bajan friend tells me they do this to eradicate the 'raw' taste from the meat, but it also helps to tenderise it.

After 30 minutes, wash the lemon and salt off and put the meat into a large cooking pot, add enough water to cover the meat, bring to a boil and cook for 30 minutes over a medium heat.

Next drain away the water, replacing with fresh water to cover the meat. Add in the remaining ingredients and cook for a further 2 hours, or until the meat falls easily from the bone. Serve as desired.

BELARUS

PASKHA
(EASTERN ORTHODOX MOULDED EASTER CHEESECAKE)

Best described as a crustless cheesecake, Paskha is a traditional Easter offering in Belarus. It is an imposing pudding that looks great on the dinner table. Often it is adorned with decorations consisting of raisins or almonds in a pattern including the letters XB standing for the Church Slavonic for "Christ is Risen." This cake which must be stored in the fridge (it lasts around two weeks) can be eaten alone or as it is traditionally served; spread on slices of kulich, a sweet Easter bread. Typically made in a Paskha mould or terracotta pot, I have made it before using a 'bowl' shaped colander. The point of the traditional mould and terracotta pot is the hole which allows the cheesecake to drain, as well as the shape, which you could be flexible on. As usual, I have done my own interpretation, whilst respecting local tradition, so you will find candied citron and cranberries (a Belarusian favourite) in the ingredients list, a slight deviation which I hope you will agree works well.

227g	butter, room temperature
275g	sugar
6	hard boiled eggs, yolks only
900g	quark cheese
240ml	double cream
40g	ground almonds
2	lemons, zest only
1½ tsp	vanilla essence
20g	cranberries
20g	candied citron peel, finely sliced
	Citron peel & cranberries, to decorate as desired

Prepare your mould/pot/colander by lining it with a cheesecloth/piece of muslin that has been rinsed in water and squeezed dry.

Using an electric hand-held whisk, in a bowl combine the butter and sugar, beating until light and fluffy. Add in the egg yolks and continue to beat until well combined. Mix in the remaining ingredients.

Fill the lined mould/pot/colander with the cheese mixture. Put a small plate on top of the mould followed by a weight. Now put the mould/pot/colander into a larger bowl to catch the liquid and refrigerate overnight. The next day, unmould the Paskha onto a pretty dish, decorate as desired, serve.

BELGIUM

CHOCOLATE & LEMON TEACAKE

It is said the story of chocolate began 2,000 years ago, when the cacao tree was first discovered in South American rain forests. Later the Maya and Aztecs experimented with the ground beans making spicy sweet drinks. Spanish explorers returned from South America laden with beans, promoting them in the royal court. Belgium was under Spanish rule in the 17th century and so was introduced to cacao, becoming the place where royalty and the famous had their first taste of chocolate. I could not resist...

115g	**self-raising flour**
105g	**sugar**
60g	**butter**
1	**egg, beaten**

Chocolate & Lemon Filling

1	**lemon, juice & zest**
95g	**sugar**
1	**egg, beaten**
60g	**butter, chopped**
60g	**finest Belgium dark chocolate, cubed**

Preheat the oven to 180°C/350°F/Gas 4. Grease and flour a 23cm diameter × 4cm shallow round tin. Combine the flour and sugar and use your finger-tips to rub in the butter. Stir in the egg to form a dough. Press the dough into the tin.

Make the filling, by combining all of the ingredients except the chocolate in a pan. Stir over a low heat until thick. Pour the hot filling over the dough, scatter the cubed chocolate on top and bake for 30 minutes. Serve hot or cold.

BENIN

LEMON FLAN WITH BANANA & COCONUT PURÉE

Sweet local flavours bring this West African country straight to your taste buds...

15g	butter
190g	sugar
45ml	water
4	eggs
700ml	milk
10g	cornflour
1	lemon, zest only

Banana & coconut purée

4	ripe bananas
50g	desiccated coconut

Garnish

35g	good quality dark chocolate, grated

Use the butter to grease a 24cm diameter × 6cm deep flan mould or glass oven dish. Over a medium heat, in a saucepan dissolve 45g sugar in the water, stir until the syrup is golden brown. Pour into your mould or dish, so it coats the bottom entirely and evenly, you have to work quickly to spread it around, tipping the mould/dish from side to side.

In a bowl, with a hand-held electric whisk, beat the eggs with another 45g sugar, then add the remaining sugar, milk, cornflour and zest. When the mixture is smooth, pour it into the mould/dish. Cook in a bain-marie for 45 minutes until the flan thickens. Allow to cool then refrigerate for 30 minutes to set.

To make the banana & coconut purée, in a blender, combine the bananas and coconut. When the flan has set, spoon the purée over it. Garnish with the grated chocolate and serve.

BERMUDA

BERMUDA BREEZE

Serves 1

30ml	**citrus vodka**
30ml	**apricot liqueur**
15ml	**grenadine**
½	**lemon, juice only**
120ml	**pineapple juice**
120ml	**orange juice**
4	**ice cubes**
Garnish	
1	**slice lemon**

Combine all ingredients apart from the garnish, in a cocktail shaker and shake. Serve with the slice of lemon floating on top.

BOLIVIA

SALSA DE ALBAHACA

Getting its rich green hue from the basil (Albahaca), this salsa, is THE local multipurpose sauce.

1	**lemon, juice only**
245g	**plain yogurt**
2 tbsp	**white vinegar**
	Handful fresh basil leaves
1	**spring onion**
2	**cloves garlic**
	Pinch salt & pepper

Combine and blend the ingredients in a liquidiser until smooth, serve as desired.

BOSNIA

TUFAHIJE

Introduced during the Ottoman rule, this is now one of the most popular puddings. Often it is served with a splodge of whipped cream on the apple's crown, topped with a candied cherry.

Serves 6

6	**golden delicious apples***
450g	**sugar**
1	**lemon, juice only**
480ml	**water, enough to cover apples**

Nut Filling

120g	**ground walnuts**
120g	**ground hazelnuts**
2 tsp	**cinnamon**
60ml	**crème fraîche**

Find a big enough saucepan to hold all the apples. Put in the apples, sugar, lemon juice and enough water to cover the apples. Weigh them down with a plate on top of them. Bring to a boil, reduce the heat and simmer for 15 minutes or until the apples are tender, but do not overcook them, they must retain their shape. When cooked, remove from the saucepan (reserving the poaching liquid) and transfer to a rack to cool.

Make the filling in a bowl, combine the ingredients and stir them until lump-free. Stuff each apple with the mixture. To serve, give each lucky person 1 apple in a dish drizzled with some of the poaching juice.

*peeled and cored and placed in lemon water (water with a squeeze of lemon) to prevent browning.

BRAZIL

LIMAO CHINA COMPOTE (CHINA LEMON COMPOTE)

China Lemons grow abundantly throughout Brazil, and the most common use for them is as a compote. This recipe came from a Brazilian friend who lovingly recounted memories of eating it as a child. It will keep for a couple of months in the fridge. Particularly tasty served with a really cold mild cheese, such as a firm Ricotta and sprinkled with freshly grated lemon zest.

25	**China lemons (or as near as you can find)**
1½ ltr	**water**
600g	**granulated sugar**
5–10	**cloves**
	Large bunch fresh mint

Lightly wash and rub all the lemons using a synthetic scourer or vegetable brush, removing any black marks or scars. Cut each lemon in a cross and carry each cut down close to the base, but keeping the lemon together at one end. Once cut, leave all the lemons to soak in a large pan of cold water (enough to cover them) for 20 minutes. Take out each lemon and remove the flesh, rinse the hollow lemon shells and put in a pan of fresh cold water. Leave the pan covered at room temperature for 24 hours, changing the water every 3 hours.

Drain and rinse the lemons once more. Next, put the lemons in a large saucepan with 1½ ltr water and bring to the boil. Cook until al dente, around 10 minutes. After boiling, remove the lemons from the pan and add the sugar to the water. Boil to make a light syrup. Return the drained lemons to the pan and simmer on a low heat for 30 minutes. Then add the cloves, and leave until cool. Add the mint when the pan of fruit has just about cooled completely and leave it there until cold enough to pour into sterilised jars and seal.

BRITISH VIRGIN ISLANDS
FISH & FUNGI (OKRA CORNMEAL & FISH)

This dish, considered the British Virgin Islands national dish, has its roots in slave women making the most of their rations, and frankly coming up with a rather innovative, tasty meal. Their rations were barely varied but always included cornmeal and fish...

Serves 2–4

320g	**frozen okra**
	Salt & pepper, to taste
170g	**yellow cornmeal, finely ground**
575ml	**boiling water**
1	**lemon, juice only**
4	**pollock fish fillets**
1 tbsp	**butter**
8	**cherry tomatoes, halved**
1	**small onion, sliced**
2	**cloves garlic, sliced**
240ml	**water**

First boil the okra with enough water to cover it in a saucepan with a pinch of salt. Cook until tender, the water should begin to have a slimy texture, taking around 8 minutes. While the okra is cooking, in a saucepan over a medium heat, put the cornmeal with the boiling water. Stir continuously for a couple of minutes. Remove from the heat and set aside to absorb the water.

When the okra is tender, remove with a slotted spoon, reserving 480ml of the okra water in the pan. Gradually stir the cornmeal into the okra water, using a wooden spatula to create a lump-free mixture. You could also use an electric hand-whisk. Next add the okra to the cornmeal and whisk again to combine. The okra will break up slightly. Throw in a decent pinch each of salt and pepper and cover with a lid.

Using a large frying pan, combine the lemon juice, fish, butter, tomato halves, onion and garlic, cook on a medium heat until the butter melts, then add 240ml of water, salt and pepper. Bring to a boil and simmer for 20 minutes or until the fish flakes easily. Serve a mound of the okra and cornmeal with the fish mixture in the middle.

BRUNEI

BEEF RENDANG

Delicious, intriguing flavours, fabulous with plain steamed rice.

Serves 4

120ml	ground nut oil
1 tsp	anchovy paste
	Pinch salt
1 tsp	palm sugar
6	slices dried galangal
6	macadamia nuts, ground
2 tbsp	curry power, mixed with 2 tbsp water
15	dried red chillies, deseeded
2	onions, diced
1	fresh red chilli, deseeded
2	cloves garlic
1 tsp	coriander seeds
2 tsp	turmeric
2 tsp	cumin seeds
1 inch	cube fresh ginger, sliced
120g	desiccated coconut, fried & pounded
4	stalks lemongrass, finely sliced
½	lemon, juice only
800g	beef steak, cubes
200ml	coconut milk

In a saucepan, over a medium heat, heat the oil and add all the ingredients, apart from the coconut milk and steak. Fry for roughly 10 minutes. Next add the steak, fry for another 5 minutes. Add the coconut milk, reduce the heat and simmer for 30 minutes or until the meat is tender. Serve as desired.

BURKINA FASO

ZOOM KOOM (SMOOTHIE)

With zoom meaning flour and koom meaning water, the literal translation is 'flour water'. The flour in question is millet flour. This is the drink used to welcome guests or celebrate special occasions, such as a wedding or a birth. Best served ice cold, with its smoothie texture, bear in mind whilst super refreshing, it is also rather filling, so an ideal pick-me-up. A local gave me the tip that it is common practice for people to add fresh mint and a drop of vanilla into the mix...

Serves 8

200ml	**water**
20g	**tamarind paste, diluted in 20ml boiling water**
150g	**millet flour**
150g	**soft brown sugar**
2	**lemons, juice only**
400g	**fresh pineapple, cubed**
2·5cm	**cube ginger**
	Ice cubes, to serve

In a blender, blitz all the ingredients apart from the ice, until they are well combined. Chill in the fridge for a couple of hours before serving over ice.

BURMA (MYANMAR)

LEMON & CHICKEN CURRY

This curry from Burma (now called Myanmar but still known as Burma by many) is inspired by a typical Burmese combination of flavours from Thailand and India, the result of its geographical position. Lemongrass; a typical flavour of Thailand, and turmeric from India, marry well, melting together seamlessly to produce a highly unique sensation for the consumer to enjoy. I like to serve it with a pile of steamed rice, noodles would work just as well...

Serves 4

120ml	**groundnut oil**
3	**onions, diced**
3	**cloves garlic, crushed**
1cm	**fresh ginger, grated**
1 tsp	**paprika**
1 tsp	**turmeric**
1	**lemon, zest & juice**
2	**fresh chillies (medium heat) deseeded, finely sliced**
1	**lemongrass stalk**
6	**fresh curry leaves**
6	**kaffir leaves, torn**
1 tsp	**anchovy paste**
460g	**chicken, cubed**
260ml	**water**
	Handful fresh coriander, chopped

In a saucepan, heat the oil over a high heat and fry the onion, garlic and ginger until the onions become translucent. Add in the paprika, turmeric, zest, chillies, lemongrass, curry leaves, kaffir leaves and continue to fry for a few more minutes. Add the lemon juice and anchovy paste, next add in the chicken. Stir to coat well in the spice mixture and add the water. Reduce the heat and simmer for 30 minutes with the lid on. If the curry needs more water, you can add some to prevent burning. Remove the lemongrass stalk and serve as desired, with a sprinkling of coriander on top.

CAMBODIA

AMOK TREI (FISH CURRY PARCELS)

Sandwiched between Thailand and Vietnam each celebrated for its cuisine, Cambodia still shines through with its Khmer culinary masterpieces. Khmer is influenced predominantly by India and China, as shown by this dish.

Serves 2

1	**lemon, zest only**
1	**clove garlic, crushed**
½	**onion, finely sliced**
½ tsp	**dried galangal**
½ tbsp	**palm sugar paste**
1	**lemongrass stalk, finely sliced**
½ tsp	**ground turmeric**
4	**cardamom pods, de-husked, seeds only**
1 tsp	**paprika**
1 tbsp	**fish sauce**
200ml	**coconut milk**
4	**large cabbage leaves, even sized**
250g	**pollack fish fillets, cubed**
2	**dried kaffir leaves**

In a liquidiser, combine the zest, garlic, onion, galangal, palm sugar, lemongrass, turmeric, cardamom, paprika, fish sauce and coconut milk until all the ingredients are blended well. Transfer the mixture to a pan, simmer whilst stirring continuously for 10 minutes or until it has thickened. Steep the cabbage leaves in boiling water for 10 minutes to soften.

In a bowl, mix the fish with half the sauce. Divide the fish mixture between the four cabbage leaves, folding and tucking in, until you have 4 tight parcels, I find securing with toothpicks can help. Steam for 50 minutes. After 45 minutes, reheat the remaining sauce adding the kaffir leaves. Serve the parcels over steaming hot rice, with a dollop of the sauce on top.

CAMEROON

GINGER JUICE APPETISER

This drink would be served with fried ripe plantain. My little cousin loved this after his Mum put it in the freezer and left it there a short while, until it had a slushy texture. Perfect to cool you in the summer heat... If you are lucky to get some!

Serves 1

2·5cm	**ginger, cubed**
240ml	**milk**
20g	**sugar**
½	**green lemon, juice only**
3	**ice cubes**

In a liquidiser, blend together all the ingredients apart from the ice, pour over ice and serve.

CANADA

LEMON, MAPLE & PECAN BREAD

Maple syrup and pecans evoke the flavours of Canada. So proud of the Maple tree (from which we get the sap, boiled down into maple syrup) Canada made the maple leaf the central theme of its national flag in 1965. This is a great breakfast bread, served with pots of various jams and butter.

55g	**butter**
225g	**sugar**
2	**lemons, ½ juice, 2 zest**
2	**eggs, beaten**
225g	**plain flour**
1 tsp	**baking powder**
½ tsp	**salt**
120ml	**milk**
100g	**pecans, chopped**
30g	**icing sugar**
1 tbsp	**maple syrup**

Preheat the oven to 180°C/350°F/Gas 4. With a handheld electric whisk, beat the butter and sugar until fluffy. Add the zest, eggs, flour, baking powder, salt and milk and blend well. Using a spoon, fold in the pecans. Transfer to a greased and floured 23 × 13cm loaf tin and bake for 1 hour.

In a bowl, mix together the lemon juice, icing sugar and maple syrup. Remove the cake from the oven, leaving it in its tin and, while still hot, pour the maple mixture over it. When cooled, unmould it on a wire rack, slice and serve.

CHILE

LEMON & ORANGE CALZONES ROTOS (FRIED COOKIES)

Translating as 'torn underwear' inspired by their shape, these cookies are far tastier than torn under garments could ever hope to be! I like to eat them whilst they are still warm. Because I have found them coming up a little dry in the past, I conjured up an interesting drizzle to drench them in, and have never looked back.

300g	**flour**
75g	**icing sugar**
½ tsp	**salt**
1½ tsp	**baking powder**
2	**eggs**
1 tsp	**orange blossom water**
2	**lemons, 1 zest & 1½ juice**
1	**orange, zest & juice**
50g	**butter**
	Groundnut oil, for frying

Chilli & Orange Drizzle

1 tsp	**orange blossom flower water**
100g	**sugar**
1 tsp	**chilli flakes**

Garnish

20g	**icing sugar, to garnish**

Combine the flour, icing sugar, salt and baking powder in a bowl. In a separate bowl, whisk together the eggs, orange blossom water and both zests. Stir the two mixtures together. Add the butter, knead into a stiff dough. Add the juice of half a lemon and knead again until combined. Cover the dough with cling film, put into the fridge for 15 minutes. In a saucepan, heat enough groundnut oil to come half way up the side.

On a floured board, roll out the dough to 5mm thick. Cut the dough into rectangles, about 5cm wide × 10cm long. Make a 2·5cm long incision in the middle of each. Pull one end of the rectangle through the incision, forming a knot shape (see the picture).

Fry the cookies in batches in the oil, until golden brown, turning them once (they cook very quickly)! Remove with a slotted spoon, drain on paper towels. Make the drizzle in a pan. Combine the orange and lemon juices, orange blossom water, sugar and chilli flakes. Heat and stir until dissolved. Drizzle the syrup over the cookies and sprinkle with icing sugar to decorate.

IKA MATA

COMOROS

LEMONGRASS INFUSED ROASTED CHICKEN

Serve up a traditional Sunday roast with a twist, guaranteed to please!

1	**whole chicken circa 1·63kg**
	Pinch salt
2	**cloves garlic**
2·5cm	**fresh ginger, peeled**
4	**cardamom pods, split open, use seeds**
1	**lemon, juice only**
2	**stalks lemongrass,**
	Small handful fresh coriander leaves
	Small handful fresh mint leaves

Preheat the oven to 230°C/450°F/Gas 8. Season the chicken with salt and put aside. In a blender combine the garlic, ginger, cardamom, lemon juice and half the lemongrass. Spread the lemongrass paste evenly under the skin of the chicken. Place the remaining lemongrass with the coriander and mint into the chicken cavity.

Roast for 15 minutes, then decrease the temperature to 180°C/350°F/Gas 4 and roast for another hour, basting frequently with its juices. The chicken is done when a knife inserted in the thigh of the bird produces clear juices.

COOK ISLANDS

IKA MATA (RAW FISH SALAD)

Most white fish can be used instead for this light and delicate salad. It is traditionally served with cooked vegetables such as taro, kumara, breadfruit or boiled green bananas. It makes a good appetiser when served alone, I like it with salad and bread as a main course.

Serves 2

200g	**fresh tuna fillet, thinly sliced**
2	**lemons, juice only**
¼	**red onion**
1	**large tomato, diced**
80g	**coconut cream**
4	**chives, to garnish**

Steep the slices of fish in the lemon juice and leave until the fish turns white and is 'cooked', the thinner the slices the quicker they will be ready. Avoid over marinating, as it will make the flesh tough. When the fish is done, combine with the remaining ingredients. Garnish with two sprigs of chives on each plate. Serve cold (you could first chill it in the fridge for 10 minutes or so).

COSTA RICA
GALLO PINTO (RICE & BEANS)

This popular breakfast dish means 'spotted rooster'. It is usually served with bread and eggs, not forgetting a squirt of Salsa Lizano sauce, if you can find it. Vegetarians, be assured there is not a rooster in sight (the name is due to the speckled appearence impersonating a roosters' plumage) In fact, gallo pinto makes a tasty and healthy vegetarian meal any time of the day. If you are having it for breakfast, you really should accompany it with the famous Costa Rican coffee!

140g	**long grain white rice**
140g	**dried black beans**
1 tbsp	**olive oil**
1	**onion, diced**
2	**cloves garlic, diced**
1	**green pepper, diced**
1 tsp	**cumin**
½ tsp	**Tabasco sauce**
1 tsp	**coriander powder**
120 ml	**bean cooking liquid**
	Pinch salt & pepper
1	**lemon, zest only**
	Bunch fresh coriander leaves, chopped

Cook the rice and beans separately, as per packet instructions. Reserve 120ml of the bean cooking liquid. Drain both. Heat the oil in a large pan and sauté the onion, garlic and green pepper. Add the rice, beans, cumin, Tabasco, coriander, bean liquid, salt and pepper. Stir together and when combined, transfer to a serving bowl. Sprinkle with lemon zest and fresh coriander leaves.

CROATIA

BLACK PEPPER & LEMON WAFERS

I have sweet memories of Croatia and not just because of the abundance of cakes and cookies I indulged in! Dubrovnik, with its intriguing limestone streets, polished and shining due to heavy footfall; most probably people scurrying towards a good spot in the Stradun to sip on a coffee, savour a cake and people watch in the Mediterranean atmosphere, makes it a place I would happily live in. Back to the wafers, they are inspired by the famous Paprenjaci (Croatian Pepper Cookies) which encouraged me to devise a twist on this classic Croatian wafer. I hope you agree, it works beautifully.

Makes 24 wafers

60g	**plain flour**
60g	**sugar**
1	**egg**
200ml	**semi-skimmed milk**
225g	**butter**
320g	**icing sugar, sifted**
2	**lemons, 1 juice & 2 zest**
½ tsp	**cracked black pepper**
48	**9 × 4½cm wafer sheets**

Combine the flour, sugar, egg and milk in a saucepan. Whisk over low heat with a balloon whisk. Allow the mixture to come to the boil, reduce the heat and continue whisking until it has thickened. Set aside to cool.

In a bowl using an electric hand-blender, mix the butter, icing sugar, lemon juice, zest and black pepper until creamy. Set aside to cool completely.

Combine the two mixtures. When cool, divide the mixture between 24 wafers, spreading nearly to the edges. Top with the remaining 24 wafers. Refrigerate for a few hours until cold and set before serving.

CUBA

MOJO (CUBAN MARINADE)

The local answer to ketchup, added to virtually anything and everything. It can also be used as a marinade.

10	**cloves garlic**
1 tsp	**salt**
½ tsp	**whole black peppercorns**
1 tsp	**cumin**
1	**onion**
1	**orange, juice only**
1	**lemon, juice only**
80ml	**olive oil**

In a food processor, apart from the oil, combine all the ingredients. In a saucepan, heat the olive oil over a medium heat until warm. Remove and cool slightly. Add the oil to the rest of the ingredients, and process again until smooth. That's all there is to it! If refrigerated, it should last for a week.

CYPRUS

CAKISTAS (YOUNG MARINATED GREEN OLIVES)

For me, these olives are required to be in a bowl next to every Cypriot dish. I love them, nearly as much as I love my other home; Cyprus. I asked my cousin Destine for her recipe, as, in my opinion her olives are the best I have eaten on the island. If for some reason she is not happy with you stealing olives straight out of her garden, any fresh green olives would do!

100	**green olives, freshly picked, stones intact**
300ml	**drinking water**
2 tbsp	**rock salt**
	Pinch lemon salt
1	**lemon, cut into 1cm pieces**
2	**cloves garlic, diced**
1 tbsp	**coriander seeds, crushed**
20ml	**olive oil**

Pound the olives slightly so they spilt (you could use a mortar and pestle, or a rolling pin). Steep in enough water to cover them and leave for 3 days, changing the water every day. This process will remove the bitterness from the olives. After 3 days, put the olives into the drinking water with the rock salt and lemon salt and leave for one week.

After a week, drain the olives, combine with the lemon pieces, garlic, coriander seeds and olive oil, stir and serve. The olives will keep up to one week outside of the fridge, if you put them in the fridge, they will last longer, however the olive oil may congeal, which would affect the taste.

CYPRUS

MOLOHIYA

Molohiya was originally brought from Egypt to Cyprus, but anyone who knows North Cyprus well, would concur it is the meal that most evokes village life, its unique aroma providing a sense of 'home'. Lemon plays a big role, and like a curry; it tastes even better the next day. Accommodating differing tastes, I make mine a particular way. Some cook the chicken or indeed lamb with the leaves from the beginning, but my method means you can cater for vegetarians easily, by removing a portion before adding the meat (in which case, theirs needs no further cooking) Some cook it with chilli, I prefer instead to serve it with a choice of sumac (a lemony spice) pul biber (more peppery) and aci biber (hotter). Serve with Çoban Salatası (Turkish salad) çörek bread, cakistas (see previous recipe) and gabbah (pickled caper leaves). Afiyet olsun.

Serves 4

200g	**dried molohiya leaves**
4	**lemon, juice only**
	boiling water
60ml	**olive oil**
4	**onions, diced**
4	**cloves garlic, crushed**
	Pinch salt & pepper
400g	**tin tomatoes**
2 tbsp	**tomato paste**
1 tsp	**organic low salt, vegetable bouillon**
500ml	**water**
450g	**chicken breast, cubed**

Combine the molohiya and juice of one lemon, cover with boiling water and leave to soak for 10 minutes. Drain in a sieve. Place into a clean bowl of cold water to rinse the leaves, work in batches, squeeze the leaves in your hands, green slime will be released, repeat this process until the leaves only produce clean water (a fair few times)! Squeeze the leaves and set aside.

In a large saucepan, heat half the oil and fry the onions and garlic until transparent. Add the salt, pepper, tinned tomatoes, tomato paste, molohiya, juice of 2 lemons, bouillon and water. Bring to a boil, reduce to a simmer and cook for an hour. Meanwhile heat the remaining oil in a pan, fry the chicken until golden and set aside. After the molohiya has been cooking for an hour, add the chicken and cook for a further 30 minutes. Add the juice of the remaining lemon, stir and serve with the suggested accompaniments above.

CZECH REPUBLIC

ZESTY BRAMBOROVÉ KNEDLÍKY (POTATO CROQUETTES)

Little balls of potato joy, serve as you would serve your standard potatoes and enjoy the crunch...

Serves 4–6 as an accompaniment.

8	**new potatoes (around 410g when mashed)**
2	**eggs, beaten**
	Pinch salt
300g	**flour**
75g	**butter**
75g	**fine dry breadcrumbs**
3	**lemons, zest only**

Boil the potatoes, they should be tender, allow to cool, skin them, put into a bowl, blend with an electric hand-blender. Add in the eggs, salt and flour, knead to make a stiff dough, it should still be a tad sticky.

In a large saucepan, bring to the boil some water. With floured hands form 2·5cm diameter balls from the potato dough. Transfer the balls to the saucepan and cook for around 12 minutes, until the dumplings rise to the surface. Drain on kitchen paper.

In a frying pan, heat the butter, breadcrumbs and zest, when golden, add in the dumplings, stirring until they are all covered with the zesty crumb. Serve immediately.

DENMARK

SKIDNE ÆG (BOILED EGGS IN SAUCE)

The name translates to 'dirty eggs', for obvious reasons, yet, in this instance, 'dirty eggs' are rather moorish. This tasty snack or indeed light lunch, is traditionally served during Easter, with a slice of rye bread to mop it up.

Serves 1–2

3	**eggs**
½	**lemon, juice only**
1 tbsp	**wholegrain mustard**
2 tbsp	**butter**
2 tbsp	**flour**
	Pinch salt & pepper
240ml	**semi-skimmed milk**
2	**slices ham, shredded**

Boil 2 of the eggs for 2 minutes, put aside leaving in their shell. In a bowl, beat the yolk of the remaining egg with the lemon juice and mustard, leave aside.

Next, melt the butter in a saucepan over a low heat and mix in the flour, salt and pepper. Cook over a low heat, stirring with a wooden spoon until the mixture is smooth, effectively making a roux. Remove from the heat. Add the milk and whisk until the sauce is totally lump-free. Return to the heat and bring to the boil, stirring constantly, for another minute; you now have a Béchamel sauce. Combine the Béchamel with the lemon juice, mustard and egg mixture, over a medium heat, stir constantly, for around 2 minutes, but do not allow it to come to the boil. Shell the eggs, cut them in half, put 2 halves on two plates. Divide the ham on top of them and add a dollop of the lemon sauce. Serve warm.

ECUADOR

EASY DULCE DE LECHE

This luxurious caramel sauce is a poplular addition to most Ecuadorian puddings and cakes. Here is my version of this sublime versatile delight.

397g	**can condensed milk**
1	**lemon, zest only**
½ tsp	**cinnamon**

An extremely easy way to make delicious dulce de leche is to simply place the can unopened into a saucepan of water and simmer for 2 hours 15 minutes. Remove the can and cool completely – that means completely!

Once cool, open and spoon out into a bowl, mix in the cinnamon and zest. It is now ready. In Ecuador, it would be eaten within a host of sweet treats, notably sandwiched in scrummy cake-like biscuits called alfajores. Apart from eating it as it is, here are a few ideas of what to do with your dulche de leche:

- Serve in a bowl alongside a fruit platter.

- Use as a delectable spread on your favourite bread.

- Top a cheesecake off with a generous helping.

- Spoon onto vanilla ice cream.

- Use as a twist in your banoffee pie recipe.

- Flavour your pastries, cakes or tarts with it.

- Use as an addition to home-made ice cream.

- Dollop into your porridge.

EGYPT

LOCALLY INSPIRED LEMONY LAMB

This recipe evokes sensations of the adaptable Egyptian spice blend called Dukkah, which includes lemon zest as standard.

Serves 4

3	**cloves garlic, crushed**
50g	**skinned almonds**
1 tsp	**ground coriander**
1 tsp	**ground cardamom**
1 tsp	**paprika**
1 tsp	**cumin**
1 tsp	**caraway seeds**
1 tsp	**fennel seeds**
1 tsp	**nigella seeds**
60g	**chopped hazelnuts**
	Pinch pepper
2	**lemons, juice & zest**
450g	**lamb, cubed**
40ml	**olive oil**
2	**onions, finely chopped**
300ml	**water**

Combine all the ingredients except the lamb, olive oil, onion, the juice of 1 lemon and the water in a food processor. Place the lamb in a bowl and coat it with the blended mixture. Cover and marinate for an hour.

After an hour, heat the oil in a saucepan, caramelise the onions, add the lamb, scrape the marinade into the saucepan also, fry until golden over a medium heat. Then add the water, reduce the heat and simmer for 20–30 minutes, when the lamb should be tender. Be careful not to let the liquid dry up, add a little more water if necessary. Add the juice of the other lemon and stir before serving.

EL SALVADOR

CURTIDO (COLESLAW)

Traditionally served with a national favourite, pupusa, cornbreads filled with cheese, beans or meat. In fact, any sandwich would do as a great partner...

450g	**green cabbage, shredded**
1	**carrot, ribbons**
950ml	**boiling water**
1	**small onion, diced**
240ml	**distilled white vinegar**
1	**lemon, juice only**
120ml	**water**
2 tsp	**dried oregano**

Steep the cabbage and carrot in the boiling water for 10 minutes. Drain and put into a bowl with the onion, vinegar, lemon juice, water and oregano. Toss the mixture until it is well mixed. Pop into the fridge for 15 minutes or so and serve cold.

EQUATORIAL GUINEA

FISH & PEANUT SAUCE

Their dishes mainly originate from the indigenous tribes, including the pygmies. This dish is galvanised by what many consider the national staple, in essence chicken doused in a delicious thick peanut sauce, reminiscent of satay. I have chosen a similar sauce, but I prefer it with fish, inspired by the logistics of the country; easy access to the vast Atlantic coast, with its surplus of fresh fish. I would suggest cod for this recipe, a popular choice in Equatorial Guinea...

60ml	**olive oil**
1	**onion, diced**
3	**cloves garlic, crushed**
30g	**tomato paste**
1	**red chilli, deseeded & finely sliced**
1ltr	**water**
2	**organic stock cubes**
½	**lemon, juice only**
450g	**peanut butter**
3	**bay leaves**
	Pinch salt & pepper
1 tsp	**cayenne pepper**

Heat the oil in a saucepan, caramelise the onion with the garlic, add in the tomato paste and chilli, sizzle for a few more minutes. Add in the rest of the ingredients, bring to a boil, reduce the heat and simmer without a lid for half an hour. Serve as desired.

FISH & PEANUT SAUCE

ERITREA

HIMBASHA (FESTIVE BREAD)

A bread that is made for festive occasions. There are many types, from sweet to salty, but they nearly always include cardamom. Although my recipe does not call for it, it is customary for a decoration of a wheel with spokes to be carved into the dough before baking.

240ml	water
400g	plain flour
60ml	olive oil
	Pinch salt
7g	yeast
2 tsp	cardamom powder
1 tsp	ground coriander
2	cloves garlic, crushed
3	lemons, zest only

Combine all the ingredients, knead well and leave in a bowl covered with a tea-towel, in a warm place. Leave it to rise for half an hour. Remove from the bowl and shape into a round disk, big enough to fit into a large frying pan. Cover again and allow to rise a second time. Preheat the oven to 180°C/350°F/Gas 4.

When the bread has almost doubled in size, bake in the pan over a medium heat for 5–10 minutes, turning over half way through; both sides should be a golden brown. Transfer the bread to the oven and bake for a further 5–10 minutes until cooked all the way through. Serve warm or cold with butter.

ESTONIA

ROOSAMANNA (CRANBERRY SEMOLINA)

This traditional home-made treat is a treasured favourite with Estonian children, an easy and tasty pudding which can be vegan if you omit the cream.

Serves 4

240ml	**cranberry juice**
240ml	**water**
120g	**golden caster sugar**
40g	**semolina**
1	**lemon, zest only**
60ml	**double cream**
1 tsp	**lemon juice**
½ tsp	**vanilla extract**

To make the semolina, combine the juice and water in a pan, add the sugar and bring to a boil. Add the semolina whilst stirring continuously (it cooks fairly quickly). Leave the mixture to cool for 5 minutes.

In a bowl, add two-thirds of the zest to the cream. Using a whisk, beat the cream until thick, set aside. After 5 minutes, stir in the vanilla and lemon juice into the semolina. Using an electric hand-mixer, beat it at a high speed until light and fluffy.

Transfer into 4 ramekins. The pudding is traditionally served still warm. Drop a dollop of cream on each serving, with an extra sprinkle of lemon zest over the top. Serve these pretty pink puds immediately.

ETHIOPIA

LEMON INFUSED BEETROOT & POTATO SALAD

Tasty with grilled meat or fish. Show someone you care about them and perform the act of 'goorsha' a beautiful tradition in Ethiopia whereby you would scoop a bitesize amount of food with your fingertips and place into the mouth of your companion, to show your affection for them...

Serves 4

½	onion, thinly sliced
2	lemons, juice only
50ml	olive oil
1	red chilli (medium heat) deseeded, sliced
	Pinch salt & pepper
½ tsp	ground fenugreek
530g	potatoes, peeled & cubed
530g	beetroot, peeled & cubed

Mix together the onion, lemon juice, oil, chilli, salt, pepper and fenugreek. Leave aside. Next cook the potatoes and beetroot in a large pan of boiling salted water for around 20 minutes, until just tender. Drain well. Transfer into the bowl containing the sauce, mix well and serve.

FIJI

SMOKED AUBERGINE & COCONUT

Shines through at a buffet, served with toasted pitta halves, also great as a BBQ accompaniment.

1	**aubergine**
	Pinch salt
½	**lemon, juice only**
80g	**coconut cream**
1	**medium onion, chopped**
6	**cherry tomatoes, finely sliced**
¼	**fresh red chilli, finely chopped**

Smoke the aubergine over a flame or even better, a barbecue, until the skin burns enough to start peeling off. When it is cooked, peel off the skin entirely and shred up using a fork. Mix together with the remaining ingredients and serve.

FINLAND

SITRUUNA SILLI (PICKLED HERRING)

A quintessentially Finnish Christmas starter, normally served with boiled potatoes.

Serves 2–4

Marinade

1	**lemon, juice only**
1½ tbsp	**sugar**
5 tbsp	**water**
5	**cloves**

Fish

2	**herring fillets, cleaned, cut into 1cm strips**
1	**lemon, thinly sliced**
½	**onion, thinly sliced**

In a saucepan, bring to the boil all the marinade ingredients. Simmer for 5 minutes, remove from the heat and set aside to cool. In a glass jar, layer the fish alternately with the lemon and onion slices. Transfer the marinade to the jar. Tightly close the jar and leave the contents to marinate for 2 days in the fridge before serving.

FRANCE

MENTON LEMON SEMIFREDDO, VERBENA GRANITE, YOGURT SORBET & ALOE VERA

This special lemony recipe is from Mauro Colagreco, a 2 star Michelin chef. It is exclusive to Lemon Compendium. If you cannot get hold of Menton lemons use the sweetest lemons you can find.

Verbena Granite

1ltr	water
220g	sugar
100g	fresh verbena
7·5g	gold jelly leaves

Yogurt Sorbet

75ml	milk
50g	single cream
25g	glucose
70g	sugar
2g	stabiliser
275g	plain yogurt

Menton lemon Semifreddo

7·5g	Gold jelly leaves
200ml	Menton lemon juice
120g	single cream
80g	egg whites
80g	sugar

Aloe Vera

500ml	water
300g	sugar
10g	Menton lemon zest
200g	aloe vera
30	mint leaves
20g	grated lime zest

Verbena Granite

Make a syrup with the water and the sugar, next make an infusion with the verbena and pass through a chinois (also known as chinoise; a conical sieve with an extremely fine mesh). Rehydrate the jelly leaves and add to the infusion. Pour into a metal mold and reserve in a quick freeze compartment. Grate the granite as it sets. Reserve in a freezer at -15°C.

Yogurt Sorbet

Boil the milk and the cream with the glucose and the sugar. Add the stabiliser at 45°C and then add the yogurt. Let it stand for one day and then transfer to an ice cream maker.

Menton lemon Semifreddo

Rehydrate jelly leaves and add the pre-warmed lemon juice. Whisk the cream at ¾ with half the sugar and mix with the lemon juice partly jellified. Reserve.

Whisk the egg white with the remainder sugar and mix very gently both preparations with a spatula, making sure that the egg whites remain fluffy. Put in cylinder molds and freeze.

Aloe Vera

Make a syrup with the water, sugar and lemon zest. Reserve. Remove the outside of the Aloe Vera and use only the transparent part. Briefly blanch in boiling water. Douse in ice water. Cut the flesh into cubes 1cm thick and 2cm wide. Put the cubes and syrup in a vacuum sealed bag. Cook at 80°C for 10 minutes and then douse in ice water.

In a serving bowl put 2 spoonfuls of verbena granite, a semifreddo cylinder piece and a yogurt sorbet quenelle. Garnish with 3 cubes of aloe vera, the grated lime zest and mint leaves.

HOT PLANTAIN CRISPS

GAMBIA

DOMODA (PEANUT BUTTER & BEEF STEW)

This stew is one of the favourites of the indigenous Mandinka people, chicken can easily be substituted if preferred, however, for this, I like to use beef. A self confessed peanut butter fan (often having a spoonful as an easy and speedy pick-me-up) I love to indulge in a bowlful over rice...

Serves 6

30ml	olive oil
1	large onion, finely sliced
900g	beef, cubed
1	chilli, deseeded, finely sliced
1	clove garlic, crushed
4	tomatoes, chopped
1	beef stock cube
2	medium sweet potatoes, peeled & cubed
1	lemon, juice only
	Pinch salt & pepper
1 tsp	cayenne
390g	peanut butter, unsweetened

Heat the oil in a large pan. Add the onions and beef and cook until browned. Add in the rest of the ingredients except for the peanut butter. Add enough water, to barely cover. Bring to the boil, reduce the heat and simmer for 20 minutes, or until tender. Mix in the peanut butter and continue to simmer on a low heat for 10 minutes, stirring occasionally. You may find that the oil in the peanut butter separates a little, skim it off if you prefer. Serve as desired.

GHANA

HOT PLANTAIN CRISPS

Although perhaps not quite traditional, I like to eat mine with a couple of poached eggs, yum.

½	lemon, juice only
2·5cm	fresh ginger, grated
½ tbsp	cayenne pepper
½ tsp	ground cloves
½ tsp	cinnamon
½	onion, grated
450g	ripe plantain, 1cm slices
	Sunflower oil

Cover a large plate with some kitchen paper and reserve. Place all ingredients except the sunflower oil and plantain in a blender. When mixed well, combine with the plantain, coating each slice evenly. Cover the bottom of a large frying pan with 2·5cm of oil. When the oil is piping hot, transfer the seasoned plantain slices to the oil. Fry until brown on both sides, turning once. When ready, arrange on the plate to drain off excess oil.

GREECE

BERGAMOT RAVANI (SEMOLINA CAKE)

I feel the bergamot adds a great dimension to this already moist, citrusy cake. A winner, every time.

Cake

120g	flour
3 tsp	baking powder
180g	fine semolina
70g	butter
190g	sugar
	Pinch salt
3	eggs separated
1 tsp	orange blossom water
¼ tsp	bergamot food grade oil
½ tsp	vanilla extract
1	lemon, zest only
240ml	milk

Lemon & Almond Syrup

270g	sugar
360ml	water
1	lemon, 1 zest, ½ juice

Almond & Cinnamon Garnish

30g	whole blanched almonds, broken & toasted
1 tsp	cinnamon
1	lemon, zest only

Preheat the oven to 180°C/350°F/Gas 4. Grease and flour a 30 × 22 × 5cm baking tray. Combine the flour, baking powder and semolina in a bowl. In a separate bowl, using an electric hand-held mixer, cream the butter with the sugar until light and fluffy. Add the salt, egg yolks, orange blossom water, bergamot oil, vanilla extract and lemon zest. Continue to mix until well combined. Add the flour mixture with the milk then mix again. Wash the beaters. In a separate bowl, whip the egg whites until you have soft peaks. Use a spatula to gently fold the egg whites into the batter until loosely combined.

Transfer the batter to the baking tray, tap it on a hard surface to even out the contents and bake for 35 minutes until golden. While the cake is baking, prepare the syrup by combining all the ingredients in a pan. Heat until the sugar has dissolved, stir and set aside, ready to pour evenly over the cake as it comes out of the oven.

In a saucepan, toast the almonds, cinnamon and zest until the almonds are golden. Sprinkle the mixture over the cake, after pouring the syrup over it. Allow the cake to cool completely (I know, it is hard) before cutting into squares and serving.

GREENLAND

GREENLANDIC COFFEE

No meal eaten in Greenland would be complete wthout it ending with one of these...

Serves 1

20ml	**favourite whiskey**
20ml	**Kahlua**
150ml	**freshly brewed coffee**
30g	**whipped cream**
20ml	**Grand Marnier**

Pour the whisky followed by the Kahlua, into a Bordeaux wine glass. Next, pour in the coffee and top with the whipped cream. Now for the theatrical bit (turn the lights down if you like for added drama)! Warm a spoon, pour the Grand Marnier into it, set it alight and pour this over the cream before serving.

GRENADA

TAMARIND BALLS

The perfect school-child snack, they grab a couple on the way home from a roadside vendor. As Grenada is known to be the island of spice, included is some fresh nutmeg. A hint of pepper is also a popular addition and, you guessed it, I have of course involved a sprinkling of lemon zest. Enjoy these incredible sweet and sour balls!

Makes 4 balls

¼ tsp	**grated whole nutmeg**
½	**lemon, zest only**
130g	**tamarind paste, pulp & seeds**
2 tbsp	**brown sugar**
	Pinch black pepper
Garnish	
1 tbsp	**soft brown sugar**

With your fingertips, squish all the ingredients apart from the garnish, together until completely blended. Form 4 balls, roll them in the garnish of brown sugar and serve.

GUADELOUPE

BANANA PIE & CARIBBEAN RUM CREAM

Guadeloupe houses 100's of varieties of banana, so much so that scientific research of the vitamin B6 rich fruit, is prevalent throughout the Caribbean island. Whilst being the main export, it provides a livelihood for most of the indigenous families, an important fruit indeed.

Pie

150g	flour
80ml	double cream
½ tsp	cinnamon
	Pinch salt
½ tsp	vanilla extract
1	lemon, juice only
1	lime, ½ juice, 1 zest
4	bananas, sliced
1	egg, yolk
20g	demerara Sugar
20g	desiccated coconut

Rum Cream

240ml	single cream
1 tsp	vanilla extract
2 tbsp	finest brown rum
1 tbsp	soft brown sugar
½	lemon, juice only

Preheat the oven to 180°C/350°F/Gas 4. To make the dough, combine the flour and cream. Add the cinnamon, salt, vanilla, juices and zests. Roll out the dough into two identical rounds, large enough for one to line a 22cm diameter × 3cm deep pie dish. After lining the dish with dough, fill it with the bananas and cover with the other dough circle. Crimp the edges to seal. Brush with the egg yolk and sprinkle with the sugar and desiccated coconut.

Transfer to the oven and bake for around 40 minutes, until golden brown. Remove and allow to cool slightly while you make the Rum Cream.

Combine the Rum Cream ingredients in a bowl. Using an electric hand-whisk, beat until thick and well combined. Serve a slice of pie with a generous splodge of cream.

GUAM

FINADENE

The local utilitarian sauce, which can also be used as a marinade.

½	**onion, finely sliced**
1	**spring onion, finely sliced**
60ml	**soy sauce**
2	**lemons, juice only**
2	**hot chillies, deseeded, finely sliced**

Could not be easier, mix all the ingredients together and serve as desired.

CEVICHE DE OSTRAS (MARINATED OYSTERS)

GUATEMALA

CEVICHE DE OSTRAS (MARINATED OYSTERS)

With its outstanding coastlines, Guatemala has an abundance of seafood, which is enjoyed daily by locals and tourists alike. This makes a great canapé.

Serves 6

24	**oysters, shucked**
4	**lemons, juice only**
8	**cherry tomatoes, peeled & chopped**
	Pinch salt & pepper
½	**onion, finely chopped**
½	**red chilli, deseeded**
6	**baby gem lettuce**

Steep the oysters in the lemon juice, cover, and refrigerate overnight. Whilst reserving the juice, drain the oysters in a colander over a bowl. In another bowl combine the chopped oysters with the tomatoes, salt and pepper, onion, chilli, and half of the lemon juice which you kept aside. Take 48 lettuce leaves, and use two to make a small bowl, nesting them inside each other. Divide the oyster mixture between the 24 'bowls' and serve in a bowl filled with ice to keep them chilled.

GUERNSEY

GÂCHE MELÉE (APPLE CAKE)

Especially yummy when served with the famous Guernsey cream or ice cream.

460g	**cooking apples (peeled, cored & sliced)**
40g	**sultanas**
1	**lemon, zest only**
460g	**wholemeal flour**
1 tsp	**allspice**
1 tsp	**cinnamon**
1 tsp	**fresh grated nutmeg**
225g	**butter**
460g	**demerara sugar**
3	**eggs**

Preheat the oven to 180°C/350°F/Gas 4. In a large mixing bowl, mix together the apples, sultanas, zest, flour and spices. Leave for 2 hours allowing the flavours to mingle and apple juices amalgamate with the flour.

In a separate bowl, cream the butter and sugar, adding in the eggs. Combine the butter mixture with the flour mix (I find using hands is best for this). Transfer the mixture to a well greased 30 × 23 × 5cm baking dish, level it out with your fingertips, and bake for around 1 hour 15 minutes, or until golden. Can be eaten hot or cold, cut into squares before serving.

HAITI
RIZ COLLÉ AUX POIS ROUGES (RICE & RED BEANS)

Essentially the national dish, an economically friendly meal, laden with healthy carbs to see you through the day, and it tastes quite good too...

Serves 4

1 can	kidney beans (400g)
2 tsp	Adobo all purpose seasoning
2	bouillon cubes
	Pinch black pepper
4	sprigs fresh thyme
5	cloves
2	cloves garlic, crushed
2	bay leaves
180ml	olive oil
400g	jasmine rice
1ltr	water
1	lemon, juice only

In a saucepan, combine all the ingredients except the rice, water and lemon juice. Allow to sizzle for 4 minutes over a medium heat, stirring so as not to allow burning. Add in the rice, stir another few moments, add the water and lemon juice and bring to the boil. Reduce the heat and simmer, covered by a lid, stirring occasionally, leave for around 10 minutes or until the rice is cooked. Serve alone or alongside your favourite meat. Typical meat would be either pork or goat.

HOLY SEE (VATICAN CITY)
ROMAN BISCUITS

The word 'biscuit' is Latin in origin, stemming from 'bis cottus' meaning 'twice baked'. Biscuits were an important ingredient in Roman army rations, as they lasted a long time and were portable. Beans also played a major role in ancient Rome, so important in fact, they were used to vote, with a white bean casting a 'yes' vote and a black 'no'. Including traditional ingredients, this recipe came to fruition...

Makes 26

360g	blanched almonds
50g	sesame seeds
400g	sugar
200g	white flour
2	eggs
2	lemons, zest only
1 tsp	cinnamon
1 tsp	nutmeg

Preheat the oven to 180°C/350°F/Gas 4. Make the all-important 'flour' by grinding the almonds, sesame seeds and sugar together. Push the almond flour through a fine meshed sieve, add the white flour, eggs, zest, cinnamon and nutmeg. Knead the dough well and divide into 26 balls. Flatten and shape them into a broad bean shape. Transfer to a baking tray lined with baking paper and bake for 25 minutes.

ROMAN BISCUITS

HONDURAS

CHIMOL (SALSA)

The perfect partner for a tortilla chip!

1	onion, diced
	Large handful fresh coriander leaves, chopped
1 tsp	salt
4	tomatoes, diced
2	lemons, juice only
2	cloves garlic, crushed
1	chilli, deseeded, finely diced

In a bowl mix together the ingredients. Serve.

HONG KONG

SESAME & SENCHA CHICKEN

My idea of introducing sencha came from a traditional Shanghai recipe which uses green tea with shrimps. Thus, this is an amalgamation with the traditional Cantonese dish of lemon chicken. Delicious with plain steamed white rice.

Serves 2

1	**egg white**
270g	**chicken breasts, sliced into narrow strips**
1 tbsp	**cornflour**
4 tbsp	**sesame oil**

Sencha Sauce

1 tsp	**organic Chinese sencha green tea leaves**
100ml	**boiling water**
2 tsp	**tapioca starch**
3 tsp	**sesame oil**
1 tbsp	**sesame seeds**
2	**cloves garlic**
½ tbsp	**light brown sugar**
1 tsp	**soy sauce**
100ml	**chicken stock**
2	**spring onions**
1	**lemon, juice & zest**

Begin by lightly whisking the egg white. Marinate the chicken slices in a bowl with the egg white, cornflour and 3 tbsp sesame oil, rubbing in with your fingertips until the ingredients are well combined. Refrigerate for 10 minutes.

Heat the rest of the sesame oil in a wok or large frying pan until it is piping hot. Fry the chicken until golden. Remove the chicken but do not clean or drain the pan. Reserve the chicken to cool for 5 minutes. Return the chicken to the pan and fry it again until golden brown (frying it twice in this method will make the chicken extra crispy). Set it aside.

To prepare the sauce, first brew the sencha in the boiling water for 5 minutes; strain it and discard the leaves. In a little cup, mix the tapioca starch with enough water to dissolve it and set aside. Using the same wok in which the chicken was fried, heat 1 teaspoon sesame oil and add all the ingredients except the remaining sesame oil, spring onions and lemon zest. Stir until the sauce thickens, add the chicken strips and stir until coated. Before serving, sprinkle with the rest of the sesame oil, sliced spring onions and zest.

HUNGARY

RIGÓ JANCSI (CHOCOLATE MOUSSE CAKE)

Part of the joy of eating 'foreign' food, for me, not only is the exposure to new flavours on my tongue, but also the immense culture and very often beautiful historical stories behind the invention of the food in question. This cake, is not only stunningly rich and delicious, it also has a delightful story behind it, making it taste even better. Rigó Jancsi was a well known Hungarian gypsy violinist. In Paris, circa 1896, Jancsi performed for Prince Josef and Princess Klara. According to the story, the Princess was instantly infatuated by Jancsi's dashing presence, and fell in love. She subsequently left her husband and children to join Jancsi, who, also taken in by her, divorced his wife. To demonstrate his love for Klara, he asked a confectioner to invent a sumptuous cake, just for her. That is how Sütemény Rigó Jancsi was born. Sadly, their love affair came to an end, but the memory of their tale of love lives on, in the form of this now famous cake...

Chocolate Cake

165g	butter, softened
115g	sugar
85g	milk chocolate, cubed
4	eggs, separated
	Pinch salt
80g	plain flour

Milk Chocolate Filling

360ml	double cream
280g	milk chocolate, cubed
2	lemons, zest only
1 tsp	vanilla extract

Chocolate Glaze

2 tbsp	golden syrup
200g	dark chocolate, cubed
30g	butter
1 tsp	vanilla extract

Heat the oven to 180°C/350°F/Gas 4. Line a swiss roll tin with baking parchment. In a large bowl, cream the butter with half the sugar until light and fluffy. In a bain-marie, melt the chocolate and allow to cool until lukewarm. Add the chocolate to the butter mixture and beat in the egg yolks, one at a time. Briefly whip the egg whites with the salt, then add the remaining sugar, beating until stiff peaks form. Fold the egg whites into the chocolate then carefully fold in the flour, you do not want to lose too much volume. Pour the mixture into the swiss roll tin and bake for 15 minutes, or until it pulls away from the edges. Cool for a few moments on a wire rack, remove the paper and leave to cool completely.

Make the milk chocolate filling by bringing the cream to boiling point in a pan, put the chocolate in a glass bowl and pour over the boiling cream. Cover, leaving to stand for 10 minutes. Add in the zest and vanilla, stir until well combined. Chill in the fridge for an hour, remove, then with a hand-mixer whisk until the volume increases. Cut the cake in half and spread the filling evenly on one half to the edges, place the other half of the cake on top and put into the fridge for an hour.

To make the chocolate glaze, in a microwavable bowl, combine the golden syrup, chocolate and butter and microwave for 1 minute. Add in the vanilla and stir until completely combined. Leave aside to cool for 10 minutes. Remove the cake from the fridge and pour the glaze over it. I find it easier to slowly pour the glaze into the middle, allowing it to flow naturally towards the edges. Do not worry about a little spillage, you can tidy that up later. Return the cake to the fridge for 20 minutes to set. This is an indulgent cake so be nice to your guests waistlines and cut the cake into small squares to serve.

ICELAND

LEMON LAUFABRAUÐ (LEAF BREAD)

Traditionally prepared to be eaten during the Christmas period, these thin breads are decorated with beautifully cut out shapes, normally a snowflake design, but you can use any desired pattern. They not only look attractive but taste great too.

250g	rye flour
8g	sugar
½ tsp	baking powder
	Pinch salt
1 tsp	caraway seeds
1	lemon, zest only
150ml	milk
¼ tbsp	butter
	Mazola oil

In a mixing bowl, combine all ingredients except the milk, butter and oil. In a saucepan bring the milk to the boil, add the butter and stir until it melts. Pour the milk into the flour mixture, stir and knead into a dough ball. Keep the dough in the bowl covered with a wet towel (as it tends to dry out quickly). Flour a board. Tear pieces off the dough and roll it out as thinly as possible. Use a side plate to cut out circles of the dough. Now comes the fun part. Use a sharp knife to cut shapes and designs of your choice into the dough, snowflake designs are the most traditional.

Add enough oil to a saucepan to come half-way up. When it is boiling, slide in the leaf breads, one at a time. Initially the bread will sink but when it rises, use two forks to carefully turn it over. The breads are cooked when golden-brown, this will only take a moment. Remove when done, and drain on kitchen paper. Repeat with the rest of the leaf breads until they are all cooked. Wait for them to cool, then serve in a stack alongside a selection of pickles, cheeses and cold cuts. Ideal for Boxing Day.

INDIA

GOAN CABBAGE SALAD WITH TAMARIND DRESSING

A pleasant salad that goes well with a fillet of fish, evoking typically Goan flavours with the punchiness of the tamarind and sweetness of the coconut.

½	**onion, sliced**
140g	**white cabbage, sliced**
2	**green chillies, deseeded & sliced**
20g	**fresh coconut, grated**

Tamarind Dressing

100g	**tamarind paste**
50ml	**cold water**
½ tbsp	**palm sugar**
	Pinch salt
½	**lemon, juice only**

In a large bowl, combine the onion, cabbage, chillies and coconut, put into the fridge.

Make the tamarind dressing by dissolving the tamarind paste in the cold water for 15 minutes. Strain through a fine-meshed sieve into a saucepan. Add the palm sugar and salt. Bring to a medium heat, stirring for around 5 minutes and remove from the heat. Allow to cool and then add the lemon juice. Stir again to mix and pour this over the salad. Use salad servers to toss the salad coating it with the sauce.

INDONESIA

SAMBAL TERASI

A condiment found on virtually every Indonesian table, this easily made, hot sauce has the ability to add a warming zing to any savoury dish. Some would simply serve it alongside a selection of Crudités.

3	**fresh chilli peppers (deseeded if you like it milder)**
6	**cherry tomatoes**
1 tbsp	**anchovy paste**
1 tsp	**salt**
1 tbsp	**brown sugar**
1	**lime, juice only**
½	**lemon, juice only**

Blend all the ingredients, except the lemon juice, in a liquidiser. When thoroughly combined, dry-fry in a saucepan for a few minutes, stirring continuously. When the sauce thickens, add the lemon juice, stir and serve.

GOAN CABBAGE SALAD WITH TAMARIND DRESSING

IRAN

FALOODEH (ROSE WATER ICE)

Typically located in any bastani (Iranian ice cream parlour) and in the homes of most during the summer. This vermicelli based pudding is said to be one of the earliest known frozen desserts and dates back to 400 BC in Persia. You can alter the taste with a variety of toppings, but it will always be a refreshing melt-in-the-mouth delight. Shiraz Faloodeh is arguably the most renowned.

Serves 4

60g	**vermicelli**
320ml	**water**
200g	**sugar**
1 tbsp	**rose water**
2	**lemons, zest & juice**
	Fresh lime juice or lime wedges

Optional Garnishes

Sour cherries

Sour cherry syrup

Mulberries

Blackberries

Raspberries

Pistachios

Mint

Put the vermicelli into a bowl and add enough boiling water to cover; leave for 15 minutes. In a saucepan, heat the water and sugar until the sugar has dissolved. Stir in the rosewater, the zest of both lemons and juice of 1 lemon. Set aside to cool completely. After 15 minutes, the vermicelli should be soft. Drain and rinse it under cold water. Once the syrup has cooled, tear the vermicelli into smaller pieces, adding it to the syrup. Transfer to a shallow glass dish and freeze for an hour, then remove and break up the mixture with a fork. Return it to the freezer for another hour, then break it up again with a fork. Re-freeze until the desired consistency has been reached.

To serve, rake up with a fork and scoop into bowls. Serve with remaining lemon juice. Sprinkle over any of the optional garnishes.

IRAQ

TIMMAN JAZAR (SPICED LAMB MINCE)

Often eaten for dinner in Iraqi households, this favourite Mesopotamian dish can be complemented with a dollop of yogurt, a scoop of salad and a chunk of Iraqi flatbread.

Serves 4

375g	**rice**
1 tsp	**sunflower oil**
400g	**lean mince lamb**
1 tsp	**ground cumin**
2cm	**fresh ginger, grated**
4	**cardamom, crushed**
1 tsp	**ground cloves**
1 tsp	**ground nutmeg**
1 tsp	**turmeric**
1 tsp	**cayenne pepper**
1 tsp	**cinnamon**
2	**bay leaves**
1 tsp	**ground coriander**
	Generous pinch salt & black pepper
1	**large onion, sliced**
900g	**carrots, peeled & sliced thinly**
240ml	**water**
1	**lemon, juice only**

Cook the rice as per the packet instructions, drain and reserve. In a frying pan, heat the oil and add the mince, spices, salt and pepper. Cook until browned. Add the onion and cook on a low heat for around 10 minutes. Increase the heat to medium, add the carrots, water and lemon juice and cook for a further 10 minutes. Add the rice to the mince in the pan, cover and simmer for 5 minutes, so the flavours amalgamate. Serve.

ISLE OF MAN

QUEENIES (QUEEN SCALLOPS) IN BATTER

A festival was inaugurated in 2009 to celebrate the succulent local Queenies, but they can also be celebrated in your own home, accompanied by my favourite tatare sauce, handed down from my Grandma.

Serves 2, as a starter

Tartare Sauce

10 tbsp	mayonnaise
1	lemon, juice only
4	spring onions, finely sliced
4 tbsp	capers
1	large gherkin, chopped
8	cooked prawns, large, chopped
6	chives, chopped
1	tomato, diced
10 cm	piece cucumber, diced
	Pinch black pepper

Queenies

1 tbsp	flour
	Pinch salt & pepper
12	Queenies

Batter

1	egg, beaten
25g	plain flour
15g	dried breadcrumbs
100ml	milk
1 tbsp	sunflower oil
	Extra sunflower oil is needed to fry

To make the tartare sauce, combine all the ingredients in a bowl, mix well, set aside in the fridge. In another bowl, mix the flour with the salt and pepper.

In a pan, bring some water (enough to hold the Queenies) to a boil. Lightly poach the Queenies until tender, drain. Dip into the flour, coating evenly, and set aside. Prepare the batter by beating all the ingredients together. Use a long skewer or fork to dunk the Queenies in the batter.

Pour enough oil into a saucepan to come about a third of the way up. Deep-fry the Queenies, working in batches of 4. They will take only around 3–5 minutes, and should be golden brown on the outside. Remove with a slotted spoon after each batch has been cooked, draining the Queenies on kitchen paper. Plate up the Queenies, 6 per dish, adding a generous dollop of the chilled tartare sauce on the side.

ITALY

FEDELINI ALICI E NOCI
FEDELINI PASTA WITH WALNUTS & ANCHOVIES

A recipe from Il Buco Sorrento, a traditional Michelin starred restaurant in the Amalfi Coast.

Serves 4

200g	**virgin olive oil**
1	**clove garlic**
200g	**salted anchovies**
1	**glass white wine**
	Pinch salt
320g	**Fedelini**
250g	**crushed walnuts**
	Parsley, generous pinch
1	**Sorrento lemon, zest only**

Heat the olive oil in a frying pan and sauté the garlic and anchovies and white wine. In another pot boil a generous quantity of water with salt, for cooking the Fedelini. Add a little of the pasta water to the anchovy mixture to dilute it slightly. Throw the Fedelini into the boiling water and remove 2 minutes before the planned cooking time. Add the Fedelini to the anchovy, garlic and olive oil mixture. Stir for 2 minutes.

Remove the pan from the heat and lightly stir in the walnuts and parsley. Serve in a large shallow dish and add freshly grated lemon zest on top before serving.

ITALY

CONCERTO AI SAPORI E PROFUMI DI LIMONE
CONCERT OF LEMON FLAVOURS

Recipe from 2 star Michelin restaurant Don Alfonso, 1890 in S Agata sui due golfi (Na).

Serves 4

Beignets

250ml	water
100g	butter
	Pinch salt
1	vanilla bean
200g	Manitoba flour
4	egg yolks (about 65g)

Lemon Cream

4	egg yolks (about 65g)
70g	sugar
100g	yogurt
100ml	milk
200ml	heavy cream
1	lemon, grated zest

Lemon Fritters

60g	flour
40ml	beer
20ml	cold water
15g	sugar
1	egg white (about 35g)
1	lemon, sliced
	Extra virgin olive oil

Lemon Sauce

5	lemons
80g	sugar
50ml	milk
80g	candied lemon peel
240g	lemon pastry cream

Beignets

Heat the water along with the softened butter cut into small pieces, a pinch of salt and the vanilla bean. As soon as the water begins to boil, remove the vanilla bean and add the flour, stirring vigorously.

Cook the mixture over low heat, beating briskly, until the ingredients are thoroughly combined and the batter cleanly leaves the sides of the pan. Transfer to a bowl. When tepid add the egg yolks one at a time, beating well after each addition and making sure that each is thoroughly incorporated before adding the next.

Transfer the batter to a pastry bag and pipe small rounds on to a parchment lined baking sheet. Bake in a preheated 200°C/400°F/Gas 6 oven for 10–15 minutes.

Lemon Cream

Beat the egg yolks with half the sugar, then add the yogurt, mixing well. Bring the milk to a boil with the heavy cream and the remaining sugar and pour over the beaten eggs.

Add the grated lemon zest, transfer to a mould and bake in a preheated 200°C/400°F/Gas 6 oven for 45 minutes. Remove from the oven, allow to cool; refrigerate.

Fritters

Place the flour in a bowl and add the beer and water in a stream, whisking continuously. Add the sugar and incorporate the egg white beaten into stiff peaks.

Dip the lemon slices in the batter and fry in the hot olive oil. Drain on paper towels.

Lemon Sauce 1

Cut the tops off 4 lemons and hollow them out reserving the pulp. Set aside. Squeeze the pulp and filter the juice. Transfer to a small saucepan, add 80g sugar and cook over low heat until a syrupy consistency is achieved.

recipe continued...

Lemon Sauce 2

Add the milk and grated lemon peel to half of the lemon pastry cream.

Fill the lemons shells with the lemon cream and place one in the center of each plate. Fill 12 beignets with the remaining lemon pastry cream and place beside the filled lemon shells. Add a lemon fritter and candied lemon peel. Nap with the 2 lemon sauces and decorate with caramelised sugar.

LATVIA

CELEBRATION CAKE

Not only rich with its cuisine, Latvia hosts many fascinating pagan traditions, particularly around Christmas. Such as a yuletide log being lumbered through Old Riga, followed by dancing and burning it on a huge bonfire, signifying ridding of negatives. In the houses children adorned by animal masks, prance around, again to ward off evil. I call this celebration cake, as it derived from sampling both traditional Latvian Christmas yellow bread and Birthday cake (Kringel). Due to ginger cookies being a big Xmas hit, I had to add a touch...

14g	**dried yeast**
400ml	**milk**
75g	**butter**
75g	**caster sugar**
	Pinch salt
80g	**sultanas**
4	**saffron, threads**
2	**eggs**
2	**lemons, zest only**
675g	**plain flour**
1 tsp	**cardamom powder**
1 tsp	**ground ginger**
Glaze	
2	**egg yolks, beaten**
50g	**blanched almonds, crushed**
	Icing sugar

Dissolve the yeast in a bowl in half the milk. Set aside for 20 minutes, then add the remaining ingredients to make a dough. Cover with clingfilm, pop into the fridge overnight. The next day, divide the dough into three long strands of equal size, for plaiting. To plait the dough, pinch one end of the three strands together with your fingers, plait them and pinch at the other end to seal. Now connect the two pinched ends, to produce a plated circle.

Leave for an hour, after 45 minutes, preheat the oven to 190°C/375°F/Gas 5. After an hour, the plait should have increased in bulk. Place it on a baking tray, brush with the egg yolks, sprinkle with the almonds. Bake for half an hour, until golden. Dredge with icing sugar, slice and serve.

LEBANON

FUL MEDAMMAS (BROAD BEAN BREAKFAST)

This dish is common to many Middle Eastern countries. An easy vegetarian dish to make if you use tinned beans, it is protein-rich, filling, and a healthy way to kick start the day. One of my favourite brunches, which I have enjoyed both in Lebanese homes and hotels. Certainly a dish where the absence of lemon would be a disaster! The tinned beans labelled Ful Medammas, can be found in most grocers nowadays. Ful Medammas is normally served with warm pitta bread. Some people mash the tinned beans in the liquid in which they are canned, but I like to drain and rinse the beans, then add my own flavours.

Serves 2

397g	**tin Ful Medammas**
2	**cloves garlic**
½ tsp	**ground cumin**
60ml	**water**
	Pinch salt
1	**lemon, juice only**
6	**cherry tomatoes, diced**
1	**spring onion, sliced**
4 tbsp	**olive oil**
	Handful of fresh parsely, chopped
	Lemon wedges, to serve

Drain and rinse the Ful Madammas and transfer to a saucepan along with the garlic, cumin, water, salt and half the lemon juice.

Cook on medium heat until warmed through. When hot, mash lightly, the texture should not be a purée, just slightly mashed. Transfer the hot beans to a serving bowl and add the tomatoes and spring onion. Top with the olive oil, remaining lemon juice and fresh parsley before serving with lemon wedges.

LIBERIA

MANGO & LEMON CAKE

Knowing this West African country, Africa's oldest republic, has an abundance of both citrus and mango trees, I devised the following recipe, complemented by other traditional local ingredients.

50g	**reconstituted dried mango slices**
75g	**butter**
90g	**caster sugar**
2	**eggs**
125g	**plain flour**
½ tsp	**baking soda**
¼ tsp	**cinnamon**
¼ tsp	**ground allspice**
¼ tsp	**ground mace**
½ tsp	**baking powder**
75ml	**milk**
100g	**golden syrup**
40g	**sultanas**
1	**lemon, zest only**
25g	**desiccated coconut**

Preheat the oven to 180°C/350°F/Gas 4. Put the dried mango slices in a bowl and cover with boiling water, until they swell, leave until ready to use.

Grease and flour a 24 × 13 × 6cm tin. In a mixing bowl cream the butter and sugar together, add in the eggs and combine well. In another bowl, sift the dry ingredients and add to the egg mixture alternately with the milk and syrup. Stir until smooth. Fold in the sultanas, zest, coconut and mango. Transfer the batter into your tin and bake for 40 minutes. When cooked it will be golden and firm. Remove from the oven, allowing to cool on a wire rack before slicing and serving.

LIBYA

CUSCUS BIL-BOSLA

Libya's national dish, traditionally shared and eaten from one large bowl, accompanied by small salads, and a host of other snacks surrounding it, for example dolma (rice and mince stuffed bell peppers). However, the dish alone, is certainly satisfying...

½ tsp	**cinnamon**
2 tsp	**cumin seeds**
3 tsp	**turmeric**
2 tsp	**dried chilli flakes**
90ml	**olive oil**
4	**large cloves garlic**
2	**large onions, sliced**
600g	**lamb leg meat, cubed**
2	**potatoes, cubed**
2 tsp	**salt**
880ml	**boiling water**
2 tbsp	**tomato paste**
230g	**cooked chickpeas**
1	**lemon, juice & zest**
400g	**couscous**
Garnish	
2	**lemons, wedges**

Begin by pounding together the spices in a mortar and pestle, set aside. Heat 50ml olive oil in a large frying pan, add the garlic, onions and meat, cook until the onions start to caramelise, add in the potato and 1 tsp of salt, stir until golden. Transfer to a casserole dish, deglaze the pan by pouring 480ml boiling water into the frying pan, collecting all the pan juices, pour into the casserole dish. Add the spices and tomato paste, stir well, cooking until the potatoes are soft and then add the chickpeas, lemon juice and zest.

Next cook the couscous, place in a bowl with 400ml boiling water, 40ml olive oil and 1 tsp salt, stir and cover with clingfilm, leave for 10 minutes. When the couscous is ready, place on a serving plate topped off with the lamb mixture, serve with lemon wedges.

LITHUANIA

AGUONU PIENAS (POPPY SEED MILK)

If you are seeking non-dairy calcium rich foods, this poppy seed milk has your name on it, as poppy seeds are known to be extremely high in calcium content. Traditionally served on Christmas Eve, in a bowl, akin to soup, swamping little dough balls called Preskuziai. I particularly like to drink it when it is ice cold, straight from the fridge.

100g	**poppy seeds**
1ltr	**boiling water**
1	**lemon, zest only**
3 tbsp	**honey**

Steep the poppy seeds in the boiling water for one hour. Tip the poppy seeds, liquid and remaining ingredients into a blender, blitz at high speed until the liquid is visibly creamy. Serve.

MACEDONIA

ROASTED LEMON LAMB WITH POTATOES

Aubergine plays a big role in the diet of Macedonians, this recipe puts a divine slant on any Sunday roast...

Serves 2–4

900g	**lamb shoulder**
4	**cloves garlic, thinly sliced**
60ml	**olive oil**
	Pinch salt & pepper
1 tsp	**dried oregano**
1 tsp	**dried parsley**
3	**lemons, juice only**
2 tbsp	**tomato paste, mixed with 60ml water**
300g	**potatoes, peeled and cut into 3cm cubes**
270g	**aubergine, cut into 4cm cubes**

Preheat the oven to 240°C/475°F/Gas 9. Cut 4 deep slits into the meat, insert the garlic cloves. In a bowl, combine the oil, salt and pepper, oregano, parsley and lemon juice. Brush this over the lamb and roast for 20 minutes.

In another bowl, mix together the remaining ingredients. Remove the lamb from the oven and scatter the potato and aubergine mixture around it. Reduce the oven temperature to 200°C/400°F/Gas 6 and roast for a further 40 minutes. Serve.

MALAWI

NSHIMA & NDIWO (CURLY KALE SALSA & MAIZE PATTIES)

This local staple is both nutritious and easy to prepare.

Serves 2

Nshima

150g	white maize meal
320ml	boiling water

Ndiwo

300ml	water
1	onion, diced
80g	curly kale, prepared
½	lemon, juice only
90g	wholenut crunchy peanut butter
1	fresh plum tomato, diced
	Pinch salt

Make the nshima with a wooden spoon to combine the maize with enough cold water to form a paste. Transfer to a saucepan and add the boiling water. Cook over a medium heat, stirring continuously with the wooden spoon until the maize is lump-free and of a thick consistency. Turn off the heat and leave in the pan while you make the ndiwo.

In a saucepan, combine the water, onion and curly kale. Cook until the onions and kale are soft. Add the remaining ingredients and stir. Cook for around 5 minutes and serve with patties of the nshima.

MALAYSIA

GULA MELAKA (SAGO & PALM SUGAR PUDDING)

*Lemongrass infuses Malaysian cuisine, therefore it just made sense to incorporate it within my take
on this customary Malay recipe. Truly a delicious pudding, not to mention an excellent gluten-free treat,
which will not leave you with a heavy feeling, should you go back for seconds... Speaking
from experience!*

Serves 6

700ml	**water**
200g	**sago pearls**
1	**lemongrass stalk**
270ml	**coconut milk**
	Pinch salt
190g	**palm sugar paste (Gula Melaka)**
10ml	**water**

Put both 700ml water and the sago into a saucepan, bring to a boil, turn down the heat, whilst stirring continuously. Cook for about 10 minutes, until the pearls are virtually see through. You will notice the water becoming starchy, rinse the sago under running water in a fine-meshed sieve.

Divide the sago into 6 glasses, put into the fridge. Bruise the lemongrass with a rolling pin. In a small saucepan, combine the coconut milk, a pinch of salt and the lemongrass stalk. Gradually, bring to the boil, stirring constantly. When it begins to boil, remove from the heat and leave aside to infuse for a minimum of 30 minutes, longer if possible.

In another saucepan, melt the palm sugar with 10ml water on a low heat. When it has dissolved, stir and remove from the heat, it should be a syrupy texture, do not over-heat or it will become hard, like toffee. Set aside to cool. Serve the sago in sundae glasses with a drizzle of palm sugar syrup and a generous pouring of coconut milk, in that order.

MALDIVES

MAS HUNI (TUNA & COCONUT SALAD)

Classic local breakfast, usually eaten with roshi (flatbread) and a cup of tea.

Serves 2

1 can	**tuna in oil, drained**
125g	**desiccated coconut**
½	**onion, finely diced**
½–1	**green chillies, finely diced**
1	**lemon, juice only**
	Pinch salt

Mix together all the ingredients and serve.

MALTA

PUDINA TAL-HOBZ (MALTESE BREAD PUDDING)

A wonderful pudding, every mouthful is a surprise, what will you taste next? A chunk of melted chocolate, a chewy sweet glacé cherry, a delectable toasted walnut, even... Absolutely delicious both hot and cold. I think I slightly prefer it cold as an indulgent energy enhancing snack, how will you prefer yours?

800g	**large Maltese loaves, (sour dough works just as well)**
80g	**cold butter, cubed**
100g	**sugar**
3	**eggs, beaten**
2	**lemons, zest only**
1 tbsp	**cocoa powder**
100g	**sultanas**
100g	**dark chocolate, cubed**
20g	**walnuts, toasted & chopped**
40g	**candied lemon peel, sliced**
100g	**glacé cherries, chopped**

First line a roasting tin with parchment paper. Soak the loaves in water covering them completely, for an hour. Drain the bread, squeezing out all excess water. Preheat the oven to 200°C/400°F/Gas 6. Tear the bread into cubes and put them into a large bowl with the other ingredients. Combine well (I use my hands for this bit). Pour the mixture into the lined tin and bake for about an hour or until golden brown. Serve as desired.

MARTINIQUE
FÉROCE D'AVOCAT (AVOCADO & SALT COD PÂTÉ)

The clue is in the name, which derives from the 'fierce' heat within the dish, due to the chilli. Once a poor man's spread, since the ingredients are locally available for the picking and salt cod is a cheap food, it has now become hugely popular. An unusual addition to any buffet, some shape the pâté in cake tins or moulds. You could also serve it up in avocado shells. A Martiniquan delight which I enjoy slathered on some plain crackers...

Serves 4

290g	**salted cod**
2	**cloves garlic**
1 tbsp	**white wine vinegar**
2 tbsp	**olive oil**
1	**onion**
2	**spring onions**
1	**chilli**
2	**ripe avocados, large**
115g	**cassava flour**
1	**lemon, juice only**
	Pinch salt & pepper

In a bowl, soak the cod in cold water for 10 minutes. Flake the cod and put into a pan with water to barely cover. Bring to the boil, reduce the heat and cook for 30 minutes (this is to remove the salt).

In a blender mix the garlic, vinegar, oil, onion, spring onions and chilli. In a bowl, combine the sauce with the flaked fish (once it has de-salted for 30 minutes) let it marinate for an hour in the fridge. When the fish is just about ready, scoop the flesh out of the avocados, sprinkle over the flour and mash together. Add the lemon juice, salt, pepper and marinated fish flakes, then mash again until completely blended. Serve on your favourite crackers.

MICRONESIA, FEDERATED STATES OF
MICRONESIAN CHICKEN

A light dish served during festivals and a local favourite which has become renowned internationally. I like to serve it with a green salad, perfect for a variation on 'diet' food!

Serves 4

380g	**chicken breast, cubed**
2	**lemons, juice only**
300ml	**beer**
60ml	**soy sauce**
1	**red onion, diced**
1	**clove garlic, crushed**

Start by steeping the chicken in the lemon juice. Set aside whilst you make the marinade. In a bowl, combine the beer, soy sauce, onion and garlic. Strain the lemon juice from the chicken into the marinade and stir. Place the chicken in the marinade, stir again, cover and refrigerate for 3 hours minimum but marinate overnight if possible.

Bake in a preheated 200°C/400°F/Gas 6 oven for around half an hour, until the chicken is completely cooked all the way through.

MOLDOVA

LEMON SCENTED MUSHROOM TOKANA

I have made this a few times for friends, it always gets complimented, so either they are being very polite or it is indeed very yummy.

70ml	**olive oil**
450g	**chestnut mushrooms, sliced**
2	**lemons, juice only**
1	**red onion, sliced**
1	**red bell pepper, sliced**
15	**cherry tomatoes, halved**
3	**cloves garlic, crushed**
2	**bay leaves**
1 tsp	**paprika**
½ tsp	**thyme**
½ tsp	**ground fennel seed**
2 tsp	**flour**
	Pinch salt & pepper
	Handful fresh curly parsley, finely chopped
	Parmesan, grated, to taste

In a large frying pan, heat the oil and sauté the mushrooms for about 5 minutes. Add the lemon juice, remove the mushrooms with a slotted spoon and set them aside.

Using the lemon-scented oil in the pan, sauté the onion and bell pepper for around 10 minutes. Tip in the tomatoes, garlic and spices, cooking for another 5 minutes. Add the flour, salt and pepper. Stir, reduce the heat, cover and simmer for 15 minutes. Return the mushrooms to the pan and simmer for a further 10 minutes. Top with chopped parsley and parmesan, serve.

MOROCCO

MINT CHICKEN WITH CARAMELISED ONIONS & ALMONDS

I wanted to make a dish that conjures up all things Moroccan, reminding me of my magical wanders through the souks. With the inclusion of orange blossom, mint, almonds and preserved lemon, I think this deliciously does the trick. Serve with some fluffy couscous, washed down with a marvellous Moroccan mint tea.

3 tbsp	olive oil
420g	chicken breast, 2·5cm cubes
2	medium onions, thinly sliced
30g	blanched whole almonds, broken
2	preserved lemon, pulp discarded, rind thinly sliced
1	lemon, juice & zest
1	orange, juice only
15g	sultanas
1 tsp	orange blossom water
3	onions, thickly sliced
½ tbsp	runny honey
6	cardamom pods, crushed
	Pinch salt
	Handful mint leaves, chopped

Heat in a frying pan 1 tbsp olive oil. Add the chicken and cook over medium heat until cooked all the way through and golden brown. Remove the chicken and reserve it. In the same pan, heat the remaining oil and cook the onions and almonds until the onions are caramelised. Turn off the heat and add the remaining ingredients, except the mint, to the pan, stir and return the chicken to the pan. Stir again and reheat on low for 4 minutes. Sprinkle with chopped mint before serving.

MOZAMBIQUE

LOCAL SHRIMP & SEAFOOD METHOD

Waste not want not – if you keep the cooking water, it can be used to make chowder or a fish sauce.

With its extensive coastline, Mozambique is famed for its delectable seafood. Shrimp Peri Peri (spicy spicy) is a favourite among the locals and sought out by tourists. It is very simple to prepare but like any dish, it is the freshness of the ingredients which make it that extra bit special. Even if you are not strolling along the beach, raw shrimps are fortunately available in many places. Serve alone, with French fries or rice.

720ml	**water**
	Pinch salt
1 tsp	**Peri Peri sauce**
900g	**raw shrimps**
1	**lemon, wedges**

In a saucepan, bring to the boil the water, salt and peri peri sauce. Add the shrimp to the boiling liquid, reduce the heat and simmer for around 4–5 minutes or until the shrimps are cooked (they would have lost their glossy exterior and be opaque all the way through; cut one in half to check). Serve hot or cold, with lemon wedges on the side.

NEPAL

ALOO KO ACHAR (PICKLED POTATOES)

Achar, meaning 'pickle' in Hindi is typical of the cuisine of the Indian sub-continent and can refer to almost any fruit and vegetable. This potato pickle is notorious in Nepal, renowned for tasting even better after a night lived in the fridge, it will keep for up to 4 days. I like it with a poached egg on top, each to their own...

4	**potatoes, medium sized**
4 tbsp	**sesame seeds**
	Pinch salt
½ tsp	**turmeric**
½	**lemon, juice only**
1 tbsp	**sesame oil**
½ tsp	**ground fenugreek**
1–2	**green chillies, deseeded & thinly sliced**
	Generous handful fresh coriander, chopped

Boil the potatoes until they are tender. Allow to cool, peel them and cut into 2·5cm cubes. Reserve. In a frying pan, dry-fry the sesame seeds until golden. Remove the pan from the heat and allow to cool. When the seeds are cool, combine them in a bowl with the remaining ingredients except for the coriander and potatoes. Mix well. Add the potatoes to the bowl of spices and stir until every cube is coated. Sprinkle with the coriander and serve.

NETHERLANDS

ERWTENSOEP (PEA & HAM SOUP)

A sign for some that the soup is ready, would be if a spoon could stand upright in it, yes, it is meant to be a thick soup. As a self-proclaimed soup lover, I have to admit, this soup certainly hits the spot and ticks all the right boxes for a hearty, warming meal on a Winter night, enjoy.

Serves 4

200g	**dried whole green peas, soaked overnight in water**
2	**carrots, chopped**
1	**lemon, juice only**
2	**small leeks, sliced**
3	**new potatoes, chopped**
130ml	**ready made, free range roast chicken stock**
120g	**celeriac, peeled & cubed**
	Pinch salt & pepper
1ltr	**water**

Ham & Sausage Garnish

2 tbsp	**olive oil**
180g	**cooked bacon joint, sliced**
40g	**smoked sausage, sliced**
2	**preserved lemon rinds, thinly sliced**
	Pinch pepper
1 tsp	**wholegrain mustard**
2	**slices organic rye bread, cubed**

In a pan, rapidly boil the soaked peas in water for 15 minutes. Drain and transfer to a large saucepan. Add in the remaining ingredients, excluding the garnishes. Stir and bring to boiling point. Reduce the heat and simmer for 50 minutes (remember it is meant to be a thick soup, so do not worry when the water gets low). Purée with an electric hand-blender and reserve in the pan with a lid on to keep warm.

Make the garnish by heating the oil in a frying pan and frying the garnish ingredients for around 5 minutes until golden and crisp. Distribute the soup into bowls, top with your crispy garnish.

NEW ZEALAND

EGG & BACON PIE

Considered the national dish, delicious and easy to make, a pie that can be served hot, or cold in your packed lunch.

Serves 4

300g	**puff pastry (can be ready made)**
½	**red onion, chopped**
4	**rashers bacon, chopped**
8	**eggs**
	Pinch pepper
1	**large lemon, zest only**

Preheat the oven to 200°C/400°F/Gas 6. On a floured board, roll out two thirds of the pastry, line a 23cm diameter, 3cm deep pie tin. Sprinkle with the onion and half the bacon.

In a bowl, beat 7 of the eggs together with the pepper and zest. Pour this over the bacon and onion, topping with the other half of the bacon. Roll out the rest of the pastry to cover the pie. Cut a tiny cross in the middle of the pie to let the steam out whilst it cooks. Break the remaining egg in a bowl, beat it and brush it over the pie lid. Bake the pie for 35 minutes or until golden brown.

NICARAGUA

INDIO VIEJO (CORN & CHICKEN SOUP)

Tortilla chips...in a soup?! It might sound bizarre, but trust me, it is delicious. Verging on a stew, due to its hearty consistency, this is most definitely not a starter, but rather a satisfying meal. Indio viejo translated from Spanish means 'old Indian'. There are various explanations as to the origin of the name. Firstly, it could be due to people originally using yesterday's leftover tortillas to thicken the soup (I prefer the texture of tortilla chips, however). Secondly – and my favourite story – they say that a long time ago when europeans came to Nicaragua, traditionaly the locals always fed them well to show hospitality. Sadly, some took advantage of their kindness and turned up regularly in large numbers expecting their tummies to be filled. As the local people were running out of food for themselves, but still did not want to be seen as bad hosts, one day, when a guest asked what was cooking, a local said with a smile, 'oh just an old Indian who passed away'. Unsurprisingly, their hospitality was not called upon for much longer, the joke worked!

1ltr	**water**
1	**green bell pepper, cubed**
1	**onion, diced**
3	**cloves garlic, crushed**
360g	**chicken breast, cubed**
	Pinch black pepper
1 tsp	**paprika**
200g	**plain tortilla chips**
20g	**butter**
6	**cherry tomatoes, quartered**
4	**sprigs fresh mint**
1	**lemon, juice only**
Garnish	
	Small bunch fresh mint, chopped

In a pan, combine the water, half the green pepper, half the onion, garlic, chicken, pepper and paprika. Bring to the boil and cook until the chicken is soft. Remove the chicken with a slotted spoon and reserve. Next, add the tortilla chips to the pan, and cook until they have been absorbed by the water.

In a saucepan, over medium heat, melt the butter and sauté the rest of the pepper, onion, tomatoes, chicken and mint until golden. Add this to the corn soup, along with the lemon juice. Cook for another 5 minutes and garnish with mint before serving.

NIGER

SALADE DE MANGUE (MANGO SALAD)

Typically found due to the French influence within its cuisine. Great with a piece of barbecued meat.

Serves 4

2	**mangos, cubed**
2	**lemons, juice only**
100ml	**apricot nectar**
100ml	**orange juice**
2	**baby gem lettuce**
4	**strawberries**

In a bowl, combine the mango and juices. Divide the lettuce to line 4 bowls. Divide the mango mixture evenly between them and top with a strawberry before serving.

NIGERIA

CREAMY BANANA FRUIT SALAD

A Nigerian friend told me that he and his brother grew up eating an assortment of fruit after every meal. He said he was particularly fond of mashing bananas and cream to top off cubed local fruits...

3	**large ripe bananas**
150ml	**extra thick cream**
1	**lemon, 1 zest, ½ juice**
10g	**icing sugar**
400g	**favourite seasonal fresh fruit, cubed**

Using an electric hand-whisk, in a bowl, beat the bananas, cream, lemon juice and zest and the icing sugar. When smooth and thick, drop dollops over the fresh fruit. Serve.

CREAMY BANANA FRUIT SALAD

NORWAY

ROMMEGRØT (SOUR CREAM PORRIDGE)

I once heard the delightful story that little Norweigen kiddiewinks leave a bowl of this stick-to-the-ribs sweet porridge out for Nisse, the barn elf, every Christmas Eve. They do this in the hope that he will be a happy bunny and look after the livestock instead of spreading mischief! However, it is not just elves who can enjoy the warmth and joy this porridge brings.

Serves 4

600g	**organic sour cream**
75g	**flour**
240ml	**milk**
20g	**butter**
20g	**brown sugar**
4 tsp	**cinnamon**
4	**small lemons, zest only**

In a saucepan, bring the sour cream to a boil, add in 50g of the flour and stir well. Reduce the heat and simmer whilst whisking constantly with a balloon whisk for 10–15 minutes or until thick. Set aside. Place the milk in another pan, bring it to the boil and add the rest of the flour, beat until thick, again with a balloon whisk. Remove from the heat, combine both of the mixtures, whisking until smooth.

Transfer to bowls and serve warm with the butter, sugar, cinnamon and zest evenly sprinkled on top.

OMAN

KAHWA (OMANI COFFEE)

The classic way to greet a guest in an Omani home. After many years of making Turkish coffee, I have a special copper Turkish coffee pot which I use to cook it in, called a finjan, however, a saucepan works just as well...

Makes 2 coffees

2 tbsp	**finely ground arabica coffee beans**
300ml	**water**
6	**cardomom pods, crushed slightly**
3–4	**strands saffron**
½	**small lemon, zest only**
1 tsp	**rosewater**

In a small saucepan combine all the ingredients except the rosewater. Stir to combine, bring to a boil and simmer for 3 minutes. Strain through a fine meshed sieve, add the rosewater, stir and serve.

PANAMA

LIMONADA (LEMONADE)

Raspadura, which is essentially unrefined pure cane sugar, has been used for generations as an important ingredient in many local sweeties, cakes and drinks. Starting life as sugar cane, it is then passed through a mill called a trapiche, to make guarapo juice. The guarapo is cooked for several hours, whilst being stirred continuously with a wooden spoon. It turns into a thick syrup, which is then poured into wooden moulds and set to make raspadura cakes.

200ml	**boiling water**
1	**raspadura cake (broken) or 90g brown sugar**
1ltr	**cold water**
10	**lemons, juice only**

In a jug, combine the boiling water with the raspadura and stir until dissolved. When it is cool, mix with the cold water and lemon juice. Give it another stir and serve cold.

PERU

CAUSA (SAVOURY CAKE)

Famous along the Peruvian coast, causa is a highly diverse dish both with respect to the filling and potato mixture. Use this recipe as a guide, but you can experiment with different versions of either. A classic variation in Peru is to use tuna and mayonnaise for the filling. In Peru, aji amarillo paste would be used instead of harissa. Sliced hard-boiled eggs are another popular garnish.

Serves 4

500g	**sweet potato**
1	**lemon, juice only**
1 tsp	**harissa**
2 tbsp	**olive oil**
	Pinch salt & pepper
Salmon & Avocado Filling	
1	**avocado, sliced**
200g	**cooked salmon, sliced**
Garnish	
16	**black olives**

The easiest way to cook the sweet potatoes is in the microwave. Wash the potatoes, pierce the skin a few times and microwave until soft. When cool enough to handle, peel the sweet potatoes.

Put the remaining ingredients except the filling and garnish into a bowl with the sweet potato, with a fork mash it together. Line a 17cm diameter, 7·5cm deep dish with cling film, layer half the potato mix on the bottom, add a layer of avocado, a layer of salmon and then top with the remaining potato mix, press down until the surface is even. Cover with clingfilm, put into the fridge overnight. The next morning, tip the causa out carefully, remove the clingfilm, cut into quarters and serve with a few black olives per person.

POLAND

MIZERIA (CUCUMBER & SOUR CREAM ACCOMPANIMENT)

The name literally translates to 'misery' because it is said that unhappy peasants devised the dish. Legend has it, that another reason could be down to the misery Queen Bona Sforza who married the Polish King Sigismund I, endured every time she ate it, reminding her of her native home, Italy, where cucumbers are eaten in abundance. Either way, it makes a great accompaniment to any meat and indeed most fish.

Serves 2

15cm	**piece cucumber**
	Pinch salt
90ml	**sour cream**
½	**small lemon, juice only**
1 tbsp	**chopped fresh dill**

Use a potato-peeler to remove the skin and cut the cucumber flesh into ribbons. Leave the ribbons in a colander over the sink to catch any liquid, sprinkle with salt and set aside for 30 minutes. Dry the cucumber on kitchen paper. Combine with the remaining ingredients in a bowl, stir and serve as desired.

PORTUGAL

ARROZ COM LEITE (RICE PUDDING)

There are many Spanish and Latin American versions of this zestful pud, this is my take on the Portuguese variety.

Serves 6

250g	**pudding rice**
480ml	**organic whole milk**
480ml	**coconut milk**
250g	**sugar**
3	**lemons, zest only**
	Pinch salt
1 tsp	**vanilla extract**
½ tsp	**orange extract**
	Pinch cinnamon

Combine the rice, milk, coconut milk and sugar in a pan and bring to the boil. Lower the heat and simmer for around 30 minutes, keeping a watchful eye on it and stirring occasionally; make sure it is not overheating and sticking to the pan. When it has reached the right consistency for rice pudding turn off the heat. Add the lemon zest, salt, vanilla extract and orange extract, stir well and simmer for another 5 minutes. Serve hot with a sprinkle of cinnamon on top.

PUERTO RICO
DRY ADOBO

Most Spanish speaking countries have their own version of Adobo. It is so common that adobado in Spanish translates as 'marinated and cooked in adobo sauce'. This utilitarian spice can be sprinkled on everything from rice and beans to meat and eggs.

2 tbsp	**lemon zest**
2 tbsp	**dried oregano**
3 tbsp	**salt**
4 tbsp	**garlic powder**
2 tbsp	**onion powder**
2 tbsp	**black pepper**
2 tbsp	**cumin**
2 tbsp	**saffron**
1 tbsp	**turmeric**
1 tbsp	**paprika**
1 tbsp	**ground coriander**

Mix all the spices together and store in a sealed container.

QATAR

MACHBOOS (SPICED LAMB & RICE)

An impressive dish, popular throughout the Gulf States, each having their own version. I use my own dried lemons (literally leave fresh lemons in a dry warm place, such as an airing cupboard, until rock solid, clean before use). Otherwise you can use shop-bought omani lemons.

Serves 4

1ltr	water
645g	lamb, cubed
6	cardamom pods, crushed
1	cinnamon stick
2	medium onion, cut into wedges
4	whole cloves
1	whole dried lemon, 6 holes pierced in it
	Pinch black pepper
¼ tsp	grated nutmeg
60ml	sunflower oil
2 tsp	ground cardamom
200g	basmati rice
3	strands saffron
20g	pine nuts
	Pinch salt

Garnish

1 tbsp	sunflower oil
1	large onion, chopped
20g	pine nuts
30g	sultanas
1 tsp	ground cardamom
1 tsp	ground cumin

Sauce

60ml	sunflower oil
½	large onion, diced
2	cloves garlic, crushed
1	lemon, juice
20	cherry tomatoes, liquidised
20g	tomato paste
100ml	stock
	Pinch salt
	Lemon wedges

Bring to the boil in a large saucepan the water, lamb, cardamom pods, cinnamon stick, onion, cloves, dried lemon, black pepper and nutmeg. Simmer for half an hour. Remove the meat with a slotted spoon, strain the cooking liquid into another container and set both aside. In the same saucepan, that is now empty, heat the oil and fry the meat with the ground cardamom. When browned, remove the meat with a slotted spoon. Add the rice to the pan, stir and toast for a few moments, then add 650ml of the reserved cooking liquid, the saffron, pine nuts and salt. Bring to the boil and simmer until the rice is cooked and has absorbed the stock.

Whilst the rice is cooking, make the garnish. In a frying pan, heat the oil and toast the onion, pine nuts, sultanas, ground cardamom and cumin. Reserve when cooked. When the rice is cooked, layer the meat on top, top with the garnish and put into a warm oven whilst you make the sauce.

For the sauce, in a pan, heat the oil and fry onions with the garlic until transparent. Put in the remaining ingredients, except the lemon wedges, stir and simmer for 5 minutes.

I like to serve the rice, meat and garnish with the lemon wedges on a big platter from which everyone can help themselves. Serve the sauce separately in a jug.

ROMANIA

MĂMĂLIGĂ (CHEESY POLENTA)

Considered Romania's national dish, there are a host of ways to make it, normally sour cream features in it somewhere, tasty with any meat.

Serves 2

130g	**polenta**
480ml	**water**
90g	**feta cheese, cubes**
2 tbsp	**olive oil**
1	**onion, sliced**
2	**cloves garlic, crushed**
½ tsp	**paprika**
60ml	**sour cream**
	Pinch salt & pepper
	Handful fresh parsley, chopped
1	**lemon, zest only**

Preheat the oven to 220°C/425°F/Gas 7. Put the polenta and water in a saucepan and stir over medium heat until thickened. Transfer to a suitable oven-proof dish and top with the feta cheese.

In a saucepan, heat the olive oil and fry the onion, garlic and paprika until golden; sprinkle this over the polenta. Transfer to the oven and bake until the cheese melts and the polenta forms a crust, about 10 minutes. Remove from oven, add dollops of sour cream and sprinkle with salt and pepper, parsley and lemon zest.

RUSSIA

RUSSIAN LEMON SUGAR

lemons, thinly sliced
caster sugar

Layer the lemon slices and sugar on top of each other in a jar until the jar is full to the brim. Store for 2 weeks in a cool place, by which time the liquid in the lemons will have infused the sugar. Use the sugar in the normal way, in tea, coffee and cooking.

RWANDA

SCRUMMY LEMON & PEANUT CRUNCH

Peanuts are a Rwandan staple often featuring in their national dishes, so I dreamed up this versitile crunch. Put out a bowl for guests to munch on, sprinkle generously over your favourite breakfast cereal/ porridge, sprinkle on ice cream, or use it the way I like it, on a serving of plain yogurt.

90g	**sugar**
140g	**raw peanuts, peeled & coarsely chopped**
1	**lemon, zest only**

Line a baking tray with parchment paper. Combine all the ingredients in a pan and heat gently until the sugar melts and browns slightly as it mixes with the zest and peanuts. Be careful not to let it burn. Once it is all well mixed, tip it on to the lined baking tray and leave to cool – happy munching!

RUSSIAN LEMON SUGAR

SAMOA

SUAFA'I (BANANA PUDDING)

This pud might not take a pretty picture but if you are a believer in 'it's what's inside that counts' you should be pleasantly surprised.

2	**overripe bananas, peeled**
1ltr	**water**
20g	**small tapioca pearls**
60ml	**coconut milk**
1 tsp	**soft brown sugar**
1	**lemon, zest only**

Combine the bananas and water in a pan, bring to the boil, then simmer for 15 minutes. Use a wooden spoon to mash the bananas. Add the tapioca, while stirring. Add the coconut milk and simmer, stirring constantly, to prevent the mixture sticking to the bottom of the pan. Cook until the pearls become transparent.

Transfer to a bowl to cool slightly. Meanwhile use a pestle and mortar to grind the sugar and zest. After the suafa'i has cooled for 10 minutes or so, sprinkle with the zest and brown sugar mixture.

SAN MARINO

PIADINA (CHEESE AND APPLE TURNOVERS)

Although the first piadina I munched on was in South Kensington, it does not detract from the fact that it is typically a San Marino speciality, and one which I adore.

Makes 4

Cheddar & Apple Filling

160g	**cheddar cheese, grated**
80g	**braeburn apple, grated**
4	**preserved lemons, rind thinly sliced**
	Pinch salt & pepper

Dough

390g	**flour**
	Pinch salt
2 tsp	**baking powder**
½ tsp	**baking soda**
3 tbsp	**extra virgin olive oil**
240ml	**cold water**
1 tbsp	**extra virgin olive oil**

In a bowl, combine the ingredients for the filling with your fingertips and set aside. In another bowl, mix the dry dough ingredients. Make a well in the centre, add the oil and water and mix until you have a dough. Knead until smooth. Split the dough into four pieces and on a floured board, roll each into a 20cm diameter circle. Prick each all over lightly with a fork.

Brush a large frying pan with remaining oil, get it super-hot, reduce the heat and place one bread in it. When golden on the underside, turn it over, place a quarter of the filling in the centre, spreading it out a little but not completely to the edges. When the other side is golden, fold the dough in half, leave for a few moments whilst the cheese melts. Do the same with the rest. Serve hot.

SAUDI ARABIA

ROASTED CAULIFLOWER IN TAHINI SAUCE

Aware of all the vegetarians out there, my take on this typical dish, with an added touch of the magical marriage between pine nuts and raisins often found in Arabian cuisine, makes a tasty meal. Serve it with rice and salad. Carnivores are welcome to eat it with meat.

Serves 2 as a meal, 4 as a side dish

1	**cauliflower head, separated into small florets**
60ml	**olive oil**
	Pinch salt
2	**cloves garlic, thinly sliced**
2 tbsp	**tahini**
½	**lemon, juice only**
75ml	**water**
	Small handful fresh parsely leaves
1 tbsp	**pine nuts**
10g	**raisins**

Preheat the oven to 220°C/425°F/Gas 7. Line a baking sheet with parchment paper. In a bowl toss the cauliflower florets with half the olive oil, season with some salt. Spread them onto the lined baking sheet, and cook on the top oven shelf for 20 minutes, or until the cauliflower is golden brown.

While the cauliflower is cooking, heat the remaining olive oil in a saucepan over a medium heat. Sauté the garlic in the oil for a minute, stir in the tahini, lemon juice and water. Simmer for a few minutes. Remove from the heat. Transfer baked cauliflower to a serving platter. Stir well then spoon the tahini sauce over the cauliflower florets. Garnish with a sprinkle of parsley, pine nuts and raisins before serving. Delish.

SENEGAL

CEEBU JËN (RICE & FISH STEW)

This classic Senegalese stew can be played around with to suit your preferences. This is my favourite combination for the dish, but it goes well with most veggies and indeed white fish, though do not omit the salted fish.

Serves 4

40g	**dried salt fish, cubed**
120ml	**olive oil**
2	**small onions, sliced**
3	**cloves garlic, crushed**
375g	**aubergine, 2·5cm cubes**
70g	**tomato paste**
4	**wedges of cabbage, about 5cm at the thickest point**
2	**sweet potatoes, (580g) peeled & cubed**
1	**white cabbage, wedges (480g)**
½	**bunch fresh parsley**
	Pinch salt & pepper
1	**fresh chilli, medium heat, deseeded and sliced**
2	**bay leaves**
1	**lemon, juice only**
1·1ltr	**water**
180g	**rice**
300g	**haddock fillets, skinned & cubed**
	Fresh lemon wedges

The night before making this recipe, soak the salt fish in water to cover. The next day, add 100ml oil to a large pot and fry the onion, salt fish, garlic and aubergine until golden. Add the remaining ingredients, excluding the rice, haddock and lemon wedges, and 900ml water. Bring to the boil and simmer for 50 minutes (the vegetables should be tender).

After 40 minutes use a slotted spoon to remove the salt fish and vegetables (do not worry if some of the liquid comes with it). Cover the bowl. Cook the rice in the remaining cooking liquid with 200ml water, until it has absorbed all of the liquid. Meanwhile use the rest of the oil to fry the haddock fillets; set them aside with the salt fish and vegetables. Serve the cooked rice on a platter topped with the salt fish, cooking liquid, vegetables and the haddock fillets.

SEYCHELLES

SWEET POTATO & PAPAYA PUDDING

Based on the local sweet potato pudding, my added twists include fresh papaya. Papaya, named 'fruit of the angels' by Christopher Columbus, is a fruit that is practically synonymous with the Seychelles, where it is found in everything from juices, chutneys, jams and curries and (similar to other countries where it grows in abundance) as a meat tenderiser.

210g	**cooked sweet potato**
250g	**plain flour**
205g	**brown sugar**
250g	**fresh papaya, cubed**
20g	**desiccated coconut**
400ml	**coconut milk**
4	**egg yolks**
1	**lemon, juice & zest**
1 tbsp	**Farina flour (potato starch)**
½ tsp	**fresh grated nutmeg**
½ tsp	**baking powder**
	Icing sugar, to dust
	Vanilla ice cream, to serve

Begin by preheating the oven to 180°C/350°F/Gas 4. Grease and flour a 20cm diameter × 9cm tin. Boil or microwave the sweet potato with the skin on until it is soft. Discard the skin and dice it. Put it into a large mixing bowl. Add in the remaining ingredients and, with a hand-held blender, combine the mixture well until it is smooth. Pour it into the prepared tin and bake for 50 minutes. Allow to cool completely, dredge with icing sugar and serve a slice with a scoop of vanilla ice cream.

SINGAPORE
CHICKEN & RICE

A fabulous dish, bringing back memories of tasting it for the first time, whilst holidaying in fantastic diverse Singapore. This meal is perfect for dinner with guests, tender poached chicken, complemented by a host of fascinating flavours, with the interest of many facets makes this a popular addition to any household menu.

Serves 4–6

5	cloves garlic, thickly sliced
	Pinch salt
5	spring onions
75g	ginger, peeled & thickly sliced
1	organic, free range chicken (1·55kg)
3 tbsp	sesame oil
3	onions, finely diced
350g	rice
	Small bunch coriander leaves
1	cucumber, peeled & thinly sliced (210g)
2 tbsp	dark soy sauce

Chilli sauce

7	medium red chillies, deseeded, sliced
25g	ginger, peeled and roughly chopped
3	cloves garlic, sliced
2 tsp	sugar
2 tbsp	sesame oil
½	lemon, juice only
½ tsp	fish sauce
	Pinch salt
1 tsp	dark soy sauce

Fill a large pot with water, add in garlic, salt, half the spring onion and half the ginger and bring to the boil. Put the remaining spring onion and ginger into the cavity of the chicken. Breast side down, submerge the chicken into the water, it should be covered by the water, turn down the heat, cover with a lid and simmer for 10 minutes. Remove from the heat and set aside for 50 minutes.

Whilst the chicken is cooking, make the chilli sauce, by liquidising all the ingredients in a blender. Set aside.

The chicken should take 50 minutes to cook (check the juices run clear after inserting a knife). Remove it and reserve it along with the garlic, ginger pieces and spring onion from the cooking liquid. Strip away all the flesh and put the meat back into the cooking liquid. Chop the garlic, ginger and spring onions finely and reserve in a bowl.

Cook the rice in a saucepan. First heat the sesame oil, then fry the onions, with the reserved ginger, spring onions and garlic from the chicken cooking liquid. When the onions are transparent, add the rice and cook for 5 minutes, then add 900ml of the chicken cooking liquid. Stir a few times, then cover until the rice is cooked and has absorbed the liquid. Meanwhile reheat the chicken in the rest of the cooking liquid so it is hot and ready to be served when the rice is cooked.

Serve the chicken sliced alongside the rice sprinkled with coriander leaves and mini bowls holding the chilli sauce, cucumber slices, dark soy sauce and a bowl of the hot chicken liquid (as a soup) on the side.

SLOVAKIA

MAKOVNÍK A ORECHOVNÍK (POPPY SEED & APRICOT ROLL)

'Best served warm with some good old fashioned custard' so says a trusted friend given a fair few of the rolls and who undertook the tedious job of testing...

Makes 8 rolls, each roll should be cut in half, Serves 16

Filling

85g	poppy seeds
½ tbsp	vanilla extract
100g	dried apricots, chopped
480ml	milk
445g	sugar
20g	breadcrumbs
2	lemons, zest only
½ tbsp	caraway seeds

Yeast Dough

7g	yeast
800g	flour
1 tbsp	salt
480ml	milk
1 tsp	sugar
110g	butter
180g	sugar
2	eggs

Topping

20g	sugar

Make the filling by combining all the ingredients in a bowl and mix until well blended. Make the yeast dough by adding the yeast to a bowl with 120g of the flour, salt, milk and 1 tsp sugar. Set aside in a warm place for 30 minutes.

Cream the butter with 180g sugar in another bowl, then beat in the eggs. After half an hour, combine the yeast mixture with the butter mixture. Add the rest of the flour, and knead well with your hands. Divide into 8 equal-sized balls and, on a floured board, roll each into a 1cm thick rectangle. Divide the filling evenly between the 8 rectangles, spreading almost to the edges. Roll each one up, sealing by crimping the outer edge. Sprinkle with sugar and bake in a 180°C/350°F/Gas 4 oven for 30 minutes. Serve warm or cold.

SLOVENIA

BLED CAKE

Affiliated with the town of Bled. A delicate cake, with a crunch.

1	**pack filo dough**
2 tbsp	**butter, melted**
220g	**sugar**
6 tbsp	**cornflour**
	Pinch salt
1ltr	**milk**
6	**egg yolks, beaten**
4 tbsp	**butter**
2	**lemons, zest only**
4 tsp	**vanilla**
Whipped Cream Topping	
300ml	**whipping cream**
50g	**sugar**
Garnish	
10g	**icing sugar**
1	**lemon, zest only**

Preheat the oven to 220°C/425°F/Gas 7. On a non-stick baking sheet, layer 10 sheets of the filo dough, brushing each sheet with melted butter before stacking on the next sheet. Prick the layers with a fork to prevent it rising. Cut the sheets into two 25 × 20cm rectangles. Cut one of the rectangles into 9 even rectangles. Bake them, spaced apart, for 10 minutes or until pale golden. Place the large rectangle on a buttered baking sheet. Reserve the small rectangles.

In a saucepan, whisk the sugar, cornflour, salt, milk and egg yolks over medium heat until the mixture thickens. Remove from heat. Stir in the butter, zest and vanilla. Remove from the heat and allow mixture to cool completely. Spread it over the filo on the baking sheet, cover and refrigerate until the mixture is set.

For the topping, whisk the cream with the sugar into peaks. Spread cream carefully over the vanilla mixture. Top with the baked rectangles of pastry. Dust with icing sugar. Refrigerate the cake until ready to serve. Cut into sections along the lines of the top pastry dough squares. Sprinkle with icing sugar and lemon zest before serving.

SOMALIA

QUMBE (COCONUT SWEETS)

This favourite street food makes a delicious after dinner accompaniment to a cup of coffee.

Makes 8 balls

240ml	**coconut milk**
180g	**sugar**
½ tsp	**cardamom powder**
75g	**desiccated coconut**
½	**lemon, zest only**

In a saucepan, combine the coconut milk and sugar and bring to the boil. Reduce the heat and simmer, stirring occasionally, for 10 minutes. Add the ground cardamom, coconut and zest. Stir continuously until the liquid has evaporated and the mixture is sticky, around 5 minutes. Transfer to a baking tray lined with parchment paper, Allow to cool slightly. Shape into 8 balls, transfer to a sealed container and then freeze until solid.

BLED CAKE

SOUTH AFRICA

BOBOTIE

Slightly sweet and spiced, with a mild hint of curry. Delicious as an interesting midweek dish, served with salad and rice. Dis baie lekker!

Filling

2	**white bread slices, crusts removed**
2 tbsp	**cooking oil**
1	**onion, finely sliced**
1	**clove garlic, crushed**
2 tsp	**curry powder**
½ tsp	**ground cloves**
2	**eggs**
450g	**minced beef**
30ml	**water**
½	**lemon, juice**
1 tsp	**turmeric**
2 tbsp	**sugar**
½ tsp	**salt**
2 tsp	**apricot jam**

Almond & Lemon Leaf Topping

1	**egg**
120ml	**milk**
1 tbsp	**flaked almonds**
	Lemon leaves

Preheat oven to 170°C/325°F/Gas 3. Soak the bread in water for 10 minutes, squeeze out the excess and crumble. In a large frying pan, heat the oil and cook the onion and garlic until translucent, next stir in the curry powder and cloves.

Break the 2 eggs into a large bowl and beat lightly. Add the mince and the onion mixture from the frying pan with the water, lemon juice, crumbled bread, turmeric, sugar, salt and jam and stir well. Spoon the mixture into a non-stick, ovenproof dish and bake for 40 minutes, or until golden-brown.

To make the topping, beat the egg with the milk. Pour the mixture over the Bobotie, decorate with flaked almonds and lemon leaves. Return to the oven and bake at 180°C/350°F/Gas 4 for 10 minutes, or until the topping has set.

SPAIN

GAZPACHO

Delicious cold soup, makes a great easy starter for a dinner party. I like to serve mine with a garnish of half a hard-boiled egg, a small handful of croutons (even better if you make your own), a pinch of salt and pepper and a sprinkle of lemon zest. Fried halloumi is also a good accompaniment, as is cubed ham, and you can't go wrong with a sprinkle of fresh herbs of your choice.

40g	**crusty white roll**
440g	**ripe tomatoes**
1	**green pepper, deseeded & diced**
½	**medium cucumber**
1	**lemon, juice only**
80ml	**extra virgin olive oil**
	Pinch salt & pepper

Put all the ingredients into a liquidiser. Blend until well combined and smooth, put into the fridge to chill. Serve with your choice of garnish.

SRI LANKA

LEMON & COCONUT, CASHEW RICE

A rice dish full of complex flavours, which marries well with any grilled meat or fish. It can also be eaten with a vegetable curry for the vegetarians out there.

Serves 2

150g	**basmati rice**
60g	**ghee**
1	**red onion, diced**
1 tsp	**mustard seeds**
50g	**cashew nuts, roasted & salted**
5	**mushrooms, sliced**
6	**fresh curry leaves**
2·5cm	**fresh ginger, diced**
½ tsp	**turmeric powder**
1 tbsp	**desiccated coconut**
1	**lemon, juice only**
	Pinch salt
	Handful fresh coriander, chopped

Cook the rice as per packet instructions. In a frying pan heat the ghee until bubbling and fry the onion, mustard seeds, cashews and mushrooms. When the mushrooms are golden, add the fresh curry leaves, ginger, turmeric and coconut. Fry for a few more minutes, then remove from the heat. Add the rice, lemon juice, salt and coriander. Stir and serve.

SUDAN

SHATA

A popular hot spice accompaniment, usually served in very small dishes alongside a multitude of other small dishes at mealtime. Diners each have their own portion to use as desired.

Serves 8

4	**lemons, juice only**
3	**cloves garlic**
3 tbsp	**red chilli flakes**
1 tsp	**black pepper**
1 tsp	**salt**

In a liquidiser, mix all the ingredients. Now it is ready to serve.

SURINAME

BAKABANA WITH SPICY PEANUT SAUCE

Thanks to the strong Indonesian influence in Surinam, Baka (fried) Bana (banana/plantain) is a popular snack throughout the country.

Serves 4

Peanut Sauce

80g	**wholenut peanut butter**
2	**lemons, juice only**
1	**garlic clove, crushed**
½ tsp	**dried crushed chilli**
1 tsp	**soft brown sugar**
60ml	**water**

Fried Plantains

100g	**flour**
1 tbsp	**soft brown sugar**
	Pinch salt
1	**egg**
80ml	**water**
2	**medium ripe plantains**
	Mazola oil for frying

First make the peanut sauce. In a small saucepan, combine all the ingredients and simmer for around 5 minutes. Cover and reserve.

Next, cook the plantains. Combine the flour, sugar, salt and egg with the water in a bowl to make a thick batter. Cut the plantain into 1cm rounds, drop them into the bowl of batter and turn them over with a fork to coat.

Heat enough oil in a large frying pan to deep fry the plantain rounds until they are golden and soft in the centre. Serve the plantains with the peanut sauce.

SHATA

SWAZILAND
SLAAI AVOCADO (AVOCADO COLESLAW)

Brightens up any barbecue whatever the weather!

2	**lemons, juice only**
1cm	**fresh ginger, grated**
2	**large ripe avocados, 1cm cubes**
100g	**peanuts, broken**

In a bowl, whisk together the lemon juice and ginger. Add the avocado and stir carefully ensuring the diced avocado is not crushed. Leave for an hour to marinate, and then sprinkle the peanuts over the mixture before serving.

SWITZERLAND

RÖSTI

Rösti was traditionally the typical farmhouse breakfast in German speaking Switzerland. Amusingly, the differences in outlook between the German speaking and French speaking Swiss is sometimes described as the 'Rösti divide', though the famous Rösti is popular throughout the country. When it came to jazzing my recipe up, I could not resist using Emmental cheese, infamous and synonymous with Switzerland where it has been produced since the 13th century, the characteristic holes are formed in the fermentation process. The name 'Emmental' derives from the valley Tal of the river Emme in the canton of Bern. With all that knowledge, I am sure you will treasure this Rösti even more! I like my Rösti served with a poached egg on top.

Serves 4

540g	**waxy potatoes**
	Pinch salt & pepper
20g	**butter**
80g	**Emmental cheese, grated**
2	**lemons, zest only**

First boil the potatoes until just cooked but still firm. When cool, peel them, grate into a bowl and season with salt and pepper and stir well (I use my hands). Heat half the butter in a large saucepan until it has melted. Transfer the potato to the pan, pressing it down with a spatula. Brown the underside, this will take around 10 minutes. Cover the pan with a plate to flip the potato rösti over on to it. Remove from the pan and reserve.

Combine the cheese and lemon zest in a bowl. Add the rest of the butter to the pan and when it has melted, slide the potato cake back into the pan, cooked side up. Sprinkle with the cheese and zest. Cook for 10 minutes until the bottom is crisp and the cheese has melted. Serve.

SWITZERLAND
GETRÄNKTER ZITRONENCAKE (LEMON LOAF)

This popular moist loaf is particularly nice spread with a little butter...

260g	**butter**
5	**eggs**
260g	**sugar**
2	**lemons, zest only**
260g	**flour**
2 tsp	**baking powder**

Lemon Glaze

4	**lemons, juice only**
100g	**icing sugar**

Preheat the oven to 180°C/350°F/Gas 4. Grease and flour a 9cm × 28cm loaf tin. In a bowl, using an electric hand-whisk, cream the butter, eggs, sugar and zest. Add the flour and baking powder and mix until smooth. Pour the batter into the tin and bake for 50 minutes. In a bowl, mix the glaze ingredients, and when the cake is ready, pour it over the warm cake. Allow to cool, slice and serve.

SYRIA

MUHAMMARA

Hammara takes its name from its red colour, making it the perfect name for this yummy reddish dip! Serve at a party with crudités, toasted pitta bread or plain crisps.

400g	**roasted red peppers, drained**
60g	**blanched almonds, lightly toasted**
3	**cloves garlic**
½	**lemon, juice only**
1 tsp	**ground cumin**
½ tsp	**dried crushed chilli**
120ml	**extra virgin olive oil**
	Pinch salt
2	**slices rye bread**
120g	**fresh pomegranate seeds**
½ tsp	**brown sugar**

In a food processor blitz together all the ingredients until the mixture is smooth. Transfer to your most attractive party dish and put into the fridge for an hour, to allow the ingredients to mingle and set.

THAILAND

SOM TAM (GREEN PAPAYA SALAD)

This colourful, aromatic salad is filling enough to have on its own, yet light enough to leave you feeling cleansed and satisfied.

Serves 4

Green Papaya Salad

460g	**whole green papaya, topped & tailed cut in half lengthways, seeds scooped out**
105g	**fine green beans, topped & tailed**
200g	**carrots, peeled & grated**
240g	**cherry tomatoes, halved**
1	**bunch fresh coriander, chopped**
1	**sprig fresh basil, chopped**
40g	**peanuts, dry fried**

Chilli Sauce

1 tbsp	**fish sauce**
1	**lemon, juice only**
1 tbsp	**palm sugar**
1	**red chilli, deseeded, sliced finely**

Peel and slice the green papaya into matchstick strips. Mix with the rest of the salad ingredients excluding the peanuts. Combine the sauce ingredients and mix thoroughly, pour over the salad, mix well and sprinkle with the peanuts before serving.

TONGA

KOKODA (RAW FISH IN CHILLI COCONUT MILK)

Fresh tuna or most white fish would be suitable replacements, though I find Gurnard works very well for this Tongan staple. For a dinner party, it looks extra appetising when served in individual scooped out and cleaned coconut shells.

400g	**gurnard fish fillet, finely sliced**
4	**lemons, juice only**
1	**onion, finely diced**
2	**red chillis, deseeded & thinly sliced**
380ml	**coconut milk**

Steep the fish in the lemon juice with the onions, when the fish has turned white in colour (around 30 minutes) it is ready to be combined with the other ingredients. Stir and serve.

TRINIDAD AND TOBAGO

CALLALOO & CRAB (CRAB SOUP)

This popular Trinidadian dish makes an intriguing starter for any dinner party. I use curly kale but traditionally taro leaves would be used. This recipe makes a soup, but in some areas of the island, it would not be uncommon to see it served thicker over some rice.

Serves 6

1 tbsp	**olive oil**
1	**small onion, sliced**
80g	**frozen whole okra**
1	**dressed crab**
540ml	**water**
120g	**curly kale**
1	**medium hot fresh red chilli, topped and tailed**
400ml	**coconut milk**
1	**small lemon, juice only**
	Pinch salt
6	**lemon slices, to serve**

In a saucepan, heat the oil and fry the onion and okra over medium heat. When onions are transparent, add the rest of the ingredients, spooning out the meat from the dressed crab into the pan, as well as adding the shell to the pan. Bring to the boil, then simmer for 15 minutes.

Discard the crab shell (if you like a bit of heat, like I do, leave in the chilli when blending or discard for a milder taste). Blend the mixture using a hand-held mixer. Serve hot with one lemon slice per person.

TUNISIA

LEBLEBI (CHICKPEA & HARISSA SOUP)

The reason to visit a hanoot leblebi (leblebi shop) is to eat a steaming bowl of this luscious, protein fueled soup. Chickpeas are one of my favourite pulses, as they are tasty, filling and nutritious.

Serves 2

1 can	**chickpeas (400g)**
4	**cloves garlic, crushed**
1 tbsp	**harissa**
1½ tsp	**ground cumin**
	Pinch salt
450ml	**water**

Poached Egg Garnish

½	**onion**
1	**slice old bread, cubed**
4 tbsp	**olive oil**
2	**eggs**
1	**lemon, juice only**
	Handful fresh coriander, finely chopped
	Handful fresh parsley, finely chopped

Drain and rinse the chickpeas. Add them to a saucepan with the garlic, harissa, cumin, salt and water. Bring to the boil and simmer for 15 minutes. While the liquid is simmering, fry the onion and bread cubes in 2 tbsp oil until golden and crisp. Set aside.

When the soup is ready, poach the egg how you normally would (if unsure, boil water half way up a small saucepan, when bubbling drop in the raw eggs and cook until the transparent whites turn white, remove with a slotted spoon to drain before serving). Pour the soup into bowls, and top with the garnishes in the following order: the remaining olive oil, lemon juice, fried bread, onions, poached eggs, chopped coriander and parsley.

TURKEY

TERBIYELI KÖFTE (MEATBALLS, EGG & LEMON SAUCE)

Nutritious, no hidden cream or stodgy flour, a protein rich and most importantly tasty meal. If you can get hold of some famous çörek (Turkish bread) to accompany, all the better...

Serves 2

2	**egg yolks**
1½	**lemons, juice only**
200ml	**free range roast chicken stock**
	Pinch salt & pepper
1 tbsp	**cornflour, mixed with a little water in a cup**

Lamb meatballs

400g	**lamb mince**
	Pinch salt
	Pinch black pepper
20g	**ground rice**
½	**red onion, finely chopped**
1	**garlic clove, chopped**
½ tsp	**cinnamon**
2 tsp	**baking powder**
½ tsp	**nutmeg, freshly grated**
1 tsp	**cumin**

Garnish

	Small bunch parsley, finely chopped

In a bowl, beat the egg yolks. Add the lemon juice whilst beating. Combine with the chicken stock, pinch of salt and pepper and cornflour. In a saucepan, heat the sauce slowly, stirring continuously with a wooden spoon for about 10 minutes. Do not allow it to boil and misbehave or it will curdle, hence the Turkish name for the dish, terbiyeli, which translated means 'to behave'! When cooked, the sauce should be smooth. Set aside in the saucepan.

Place all the meatball ingredients in a large bowl, and knead for 5–10 minutes with your hands. The mixture should be as smooth as possible (sometimes, I use an electric hand-blender). When well combined form walnut sized balls from the mixture. Half fill a saucepan with water and bring to the boil. Transfer the balls to the pan and simmer for about 20 minutes. Remove the meatballs from the water with a slotted spoon and add to the sauce. Heat very gently for a few minutes and serve with rice and a chunk of bread of your choice. Garnish with fresh parsley before serving. Afiyet olsun!

TURKEY

AŞURE (NOAH'S PUDDING)

This is one of my favourite Turkish puddings. The name in Turkish derives from the Arabic word aşr, meaning ten, referring to the tenth day of the month of Muharram, the first month of the lunar year and a day associated with the death of the Prophet Muhammed's grandson Hussein; this delicious and attractive pudding is served in his memory. The English name derives from a belief that the pudding was created when Noah's Ark finally hit land, inspiring the survivors to cook up a celebratory treat from the remaining supplies.

1½ltr	water
100g	pearl barley
140g	cooked chickpeas, rinsed and drained
140g	cooked white beans, rinsed and drained
1 tbsp	rice
100g	dried figs, chopped
40g	sultanas
40g	dried cranberries
80g	dried apricots, chopped
200g	sugar
1 tsp	rosewater
1	lemon, juice only
Pomegranate & Nut Garnish	
1	pomegranate
2 tbsp	ground cinnamon
100g	walnuts, broken into pieces
1 tbsp	currants
1 tbsp	pine nuts
80g	hazelnuts, chopped
100g	blanched almonds, chopped
2	lemons, zest only

Heat 1 litre of the water and cook the pearl barley in a large saucepan. Cook until very tender, around 20 minutes. Add the chickpeas, beans, rice, the rest of the water, figs, sultanas, cranberries, apricots and sugar. Bring to the boil, reduce to a simmer and cook for 50 minutes. Add the rosewater and lemon juice and stir. Decant into serving dishes.

Remove the seeds from the pomegranate, being careful to discard the bitter pith. Combine with the rest of the garnish ingredients and sprinkle this over the top of the pudding. Serve hot or cold.

UKRAINE

BERGAMOT GLAZED MAKIWNYK
(CHRISTMAS EVE POPPY SEED CAKE)

A delightful cake, of course any Ukrainian will tell you the traditional recipe does not call for bergamot, that said, hopefully most would agree, the addition makes a nice surprise. Enjoy alone or with some fruit compote.

100g	poppy seeds
230ml	milk
30g	cornflour
100ml	light olive oil
50g	sugar
1	lemon, ½ juice, whole zest
120g	flour
1 tsp	cinnamon
1 tbsp	baking powder

Bergamot Glaze

30ml	fresh bergamot juice
20g	sugar
½ tsp	ground ginger

Soak the poppy seeds in the milk for an hour. Preheat the oven to 180°C/350°F/Gas 4. In a bowl, combine the remaining cake ingredients with the poppy seed/milk mixture. Transfer to a greased 20cm diameter × 8cm cake tin, with a removable bottom. Bake for 40 minutes.

Whilst the cake is cooking prepare the glaze. In a saucepan, combine and heat the glaze ingredients together until the sugar dissolves, it should be poured over the cake immediately once you have removed it from the oven, allow to cool before serving.

UNITED ARAB EMIRATES

AL BATHEETH (DATE SWEET)

Popular Emirati sweets, serve to guests accompanying some tea or coffee...

Makes 12

115g	**wholewheat flour**
45g	**ghee**
½ tsp	**ground cardamom**
150g	**soft dates, pitted finely chopped**
1	**lemon, zest only**
1 tbsp	**icing sugar**

Over a medium heat, cook the flour in a saucepan, for around 8 minutes until brown. In a separate pan, over a medium heat, melt the ghee with the cardamom, stirring for around 5 minutes, set aside.

Combine the dates with the flour and continue to heat whilst stirring until the mixture is soft. Add the zest and stir again. Mix the ghee with the date mixture and leave to cool. Make 12-oval shaped sweets, dust with icing sugar and serve.

UNITED KINGDOM, ENGLAND

CUCUMBER SANDWICH

Quintessentially English, light, moreish, even better when washed down with a nice cup of tea. If you have one, use your finest English chintz tea set to serve...

Makes 30 fingers

1	**medium cucumber, peeled**
	Pinch salt & pepper
110g	**softened butter**
	Small handful fresh mint leaves, finely chopped
½	**lemon, juice only**
1 tsp	**paprika**
1 loaf	**fresh white loaf, thinly sliced**
	Mint sprigs, for garnish

Slice the cucumber paper thin. Place it in a colander, sprinkle with salt and leave for 20 minutes. In a bowl, mix together the butter, mint, lemon juice, paprika and a pinch of salt & pepper, until smooth.

Divide the bread slices into two piles. Spread one evenly with the butter mixture, top with a couple of layers of cucumber and cover with the other piece of plain bread. Trim all of the crusts off as neatly as you can, ensuring you have straight edges. Next slice the sandwiches into 3 rectangles to make 3 sandwich fingers. Display attractively on a serving dish, garnished with a few sprigs of mint.

UNITED KINGDOM, ENGLAND
LIVERPOOL TART

320g	**ready made sheet, shortcrust pastry**
55g	**butter**
225g	**dark muscovado sugar**
1	**lemon, juice only**
1	**egg**

Preheat your oven to 190°C/375°F/Gas 5. Line a greased and floured 22cm diameter × 5cm deep tart tin with the rolled out pastry. In a saucepan, melt together the butter and sugar. Stir then remove from the heat and allow to cool. Cut the lemon into wedges, allowing you to remove all the pips.

In a food processor, blitz together the sugar and butter mixture, egg and lemon wedges until smooth and combined. Transfer the mixture into the lined tart tin and bake for 20 minutes. Serve hot or cold.

UNITED KINGDOM, IRELAND
BARMBRACK (CELTIC TEA BREAD)

Also known as Báirín Breac, this fruity, dense tea bread, is a highlight of Irish Halloween. Steeped in intriguing tradition, the baker would drop into the cake mix before baking, meaningful charms, part of the joy in eating the bread would be to discover this special charm within your slice. Charms include; a coin (signifying future wealth) a rag (financial instability ahead) a ring (Mum needs to buy a hat, as it means you will be married within a year) a pea (put that hat in the closet, you will not be married in the coming year) a stick (if you are married, you are doomed for unhappiness or continual arguments). If you are thinking of following this tradition, remember to thoroughly disinfect each item and wrap it in a little piece of greaseproof paper before adding to the cake.

Rich Fruit Cake

260g	**mixed candied peel, finely chopped**
3	**lemons, juice only**
230g	**self raising flour**
1	**egg, beaten**
130g	**soft brown sugar**

Cinnamon Topping

20g	**butter**
1 tsp	**cinnamon**
1 tsp	**ground coriander**
1 tbsp	**maple syrup**

Soak the peel in the lemon juice for an hour. Combine with the rest of the ingredients and mix well.

Preheat the oven to 180°C/350°F/Gas 4. Grease a 20cm diameter × 4cm cake tin, with a removable bottom. Pour the cake batter in the tin and bake for 45 minutes.

Meanwhile combine the topping ingredients. As soon as you remove the cake from the oven, pour the cinnamon topping over it. Serve the cake when completely cool, it is a winner for any grown-up tea party.

UNITED KINGDOM, SCOTLAND
KALE BROSE (KALE SOUP)

A soup that would be fun to serve on halloween due to its deep green hue. Extremely healthy being high in iron, thanks to the Scottish staple that is curly kale, and the comforting, cholesterol lowering, oats.

2ltr	**vegetable stock**
70g	**curly kale, stalks removed & shredded**
60g	**Scottish oats**
1	**lemon, ½ juice & whole zest**
	Glug olive oil
2	**rashers smoked bacon, cut into small pieces**
	Pinch salt & pepper

Fill a saucepan with the vegetable stock and prepared curly kale. Bring to a boil, cook for 5 minutes. Combine 40g oats, and lemon juice in a bowl, transfer to the kale broth. Cook together for 5 minutes.

Heat the olive oil in a small saucepan, add the reserved oats, bacon, pinch of salt & pepper, lemon zest and fry until golden. Pour the brose into bowls and top with toasted zesty oat mix.

UNITED KINGDOM, WALES
LIMONCELLO WELSH RAREBIT/RABBIT
(POSH CHEESE ON TOAST)

Welsh rarebit is mentioned as far back as 1547 in Andre Borde's Fyrste Boke of the Introduction of Knowledge. The name of the dish has been debated by many, one argument is that the 'rare' part would allude to the fact it is not a dish to be cooked for a very long time and the 'bit' could frankly be because it is intended as a snack or a light bite (bit) to eat. Conversely, it is disputed the correct name is Welsh Rabbit and that the rarebit version happened due to Chinese whispers. It has also been debated that it is a sign of the Welsh sense of humour in times of austerity, when they could not have even eaten rabbit even if they had wanted to. The meal in that case, has been put down to something that was concocted after a hunt returned empty handed. Naturally with a penchant for lemon, I experimented with changing the customary beer ingredient, instead dabbling with some fine Limoncello left over from a trip to Italy. Happily, it turned out well and I am pleased to share it with you...

Serves 4

50g	butter
50g	flour
120ml	Limoncello
220g	strong cheddar, grated
1 tsp	English mustard
2 tsp	Worcestershire sauce
	Pinch of black pepper
4	slices granary bread
1	lemon, zest only

Melt the butter in a saucepan. Add the flour and stir to make a roux, stirring continually for a few moments to prevent burning. Slowly stir in the Limoncello until the mixture has the consistency of a smooth sauce. Add the grated cheese and mix until melted. The sauce should have a thick texture, use a balloon whisk to help it along. When smooth, add the remaining ingredients except the bread and zest.

Toast the bread, top with the cheese mixture and place under a hot grill until golden brown. Divide the zest between the slices before serving.

URUGUAY

FAINÁ (CHICKPEA FLATBREAD)

This perfect gluten-free bread, reminds me of the 'socca' I hunted down to eat in Nice; France, as it is a local speciality. A slice of fainá is often eaten topped with a pizza slice, this is called 'pizza a caballo', translating to 'horseback pizza'.

Serves 6

220g	**chickpea flour**
½ tsp	**salt**
1 tsp	**pepper**
100ml	**olive oil**
2	**lemons, zest only**
400ml	**water**

Combine the chickpea flour, salt and pepper, 40ml olive oil and the zest in a bowl, blend with an electric hand-held mixer. Add the water, whisking until combined. Set aside for 30 minutes.

Preheat the oven to 230°C/450°F/Gas 8. Pour the rest of the olive oil into a 25cm diameter × 2·5cm tart tin. Put the pan in the oven until the oil boils, around 5 minutes. Remove the tart tin from the oven (be careful)! Pour the batter into it and return to the oven. Bake for around 15 minutes or until golden.

VANUATU

NALOT (BANANA PUDDING)

Nalot is a classic dish made using taro, breadfruit or banana, mixed with creamed coconut. This version is loosely based on the original recipe. I like to make this as a treat to eat in the winter months, it is both warming and delicious.

Serves 1

2	**ripe bananas, mashed**
2 tbsp	**desiccated coconut**
½	**lemon, juice only**
50g	**creamed coconut**

Simply combine all ingredients, heat in a small saucepan and serve.

VIETNAM

PHO BO (RICE NOODLE & BEEF SOUP)

Considered the national dish of Vietnam, much more than a soup, this lemongrass infused delight not only satisfies but is quick, easy to produce and healthy. A highly versatile soup to suit anyone, the beef can be substituted for tofu, prawns or paper-thin strips of chicken. So why not give this classic Vietnamese staple a try...

Serves 4

160g	**dry rice noodles**
1 tsp	**brown sugar**
1 tsp	**soy sauce**
2 tsp	**fish sauce**
	Pinch salt
¼ tsp	**black pepper corns, crushed**
300g	**fresh free range roast chicken stock**
1cm	**cube fresh ginger, sliced thinly**
½	**lime, juice only**
½	**lemon, juice only**
1	**lemongrass stalk, sliced thinly**
1	**cinnamon stick**
2	**baby pak choi, sliced**
1	**green chilli, deseeded, sliced thinly**
600ml	**water**
340g	**lean beef, thinly sliced**
3 tbsp	**sunflower oil**

Green Garnish

	Handful fresh coriander
	Handful beansprouts
4	**spring onions, sliced**
1	**lemon, wedges**

Fill a large bowl with boiling water. Submerge the rice noodles in it, and leave them to soften. In a saucepan, bring the remaining ingredients, apart from beef, oil and garnishes, to the boil. Simmer for 10 minutes, then add in the rice noodles and cook for a further 5 minutes.

Whilst the liquid is simmering, heat the oil in a frying pan until piping hot. Flash fry the beef slices until cooked all the way through, it should not take long (some recipes even suggest serving them raw over the soup). When the beef is ready, distribute the broth evenly between bowls, so everyone gets some of all the ingredients, then distribute the beef and garnishes between the portions.

WEST BANK

MUSAKHAN

Serves 4

2	**onions, thinly sliced**
220ml	**olive oil**
1	**lemon, juice only**
3	**saffron threads**
3 tbsp	**sumac**
1 tbsp	**allspice**
600g	**chicken breast, cubed**
120ml	**water**
4	**pitta breads**
50g	**slivered almonds**
2 tbsp	**pine nuts**

Preheat the oven to 180°C/350°F/Gas 4. Combine the onion with 120ml olive oil, lemon juice, saffron, sumac and allspice. Cover the bottom of a lined baking dish with a layer of half the onion mix. Arrange the chicken pieces on top and cover the chicken with the remaining onions. Pour the water over the mixture and bake for 45 minutes, until the chicken is golden brown.

Use 80ml of the olive oil to grease another baking tray. Lay the pitta on the bottom and top with the cooked chicken pieces and onions, plus about 3 tbsp of the chicken liquids. Cook for a further 15 minutes. Meanwhile, fry the almond slivers and pine nuts in 20ml of olive oil, leave aside. Garnish the pitta breads with the almond and pine nuts before serving.

YEMEN

YEMENITE CHAROSET

This sweet mixture which is served at Passover commemorates the mortar which the Hebrew slaves used to bind the bricks together.

Serves 24

½ cup	**blanched almonds**
8	**dried dates, pitted**
8	**dried figs**
1 tsp	**ground ginger**
1 tsp	**ground coriander**
1	**lemon, grated zest**
1 tbsp	**honey**
60ml	**sweet white wine**
¼ tsp	**cayenne pepper**
30g	**toasted sesame seeds**

Place all the ingredients except the sesame seeds in a food processor and process them until smooth. Put into the fridge for an hour. Form 2·5cm diameter balls from the mixture and roll in the sesame seeds, coating evenly. Serve.

ZAMBIA

ZAMBIAN PIRI PIRI

Native piri piri (pepper pepper) chillies, are also known as African birds eye chilli and are the main star in this fiery condiment...

80ml	**olive oil**
4	**piri piri chillies, thinly sliced**
2	**lemons, juice only**
1 tsp	**salt**
1 tsp	**garlic powder**

In a saucepan, heat 20ml olive oil and fry the chillies until mushy. Remove from the heat and allow them to cool. Combine with the other ingredients in a blender, blitz until smooth, serve in ramekins.

ZIMBABWE

BOTA (ZIMBABWEAN PORRIDGE)

For someone who is very adventurous with food, I would happily eat porridge with a variety of toppings, for EVERY breakfast, this however, might just creep in as an exception...

Serves 2

130g	**white maize meal**
840ml	**water**
20g	**butter**
1	**lemon, juice only**
2 tbsp	**soft brown sugar**

In a saucepan place the maize with 120ml water and use a wooden spoon to mix to a thick paste. Add 720ml water and simmer for 15 minutes, stirring occasionally, so the porridge is smooth. When the porridge is cooked, add in the butter, lemon juice and sugar. Give it one last stir and serve.

CONVERSION TABLES

To master becoming a fine multicultural lemony chef in no time whatsoever, remember, a tad too much or a smidgeon too little of an ingredient will not make a huge difference, so go with your gut instinct and have fun, whilst trying to keep within the guidelines.

A pint isn't always a pint: in British, Australian and certain Canadian recipes you'll see an imperial pint listed as 20 fluid ounces. American and some Canadian recipes use the American pint measurement, which is 16 fluid ounces. 1 quart (liquid) is equal to 2 British pints.

To convert Fahrenheit to Celsius: subtract 32 from the Fahrenheit measure and divide by 1·8.

When using a fan oven, you will need to reduce the oven temperature by 20°C/50°F.

All spoon measurements are level, unless specified otherwise.

All butter is unsalted, unless specified otherwise.

Where eggs are mentioned, use organic free range standard size, unless stated otherwise.

Use granulated sugar unless stated otherwise.

When a recipe calls for juice and zest, zest the lemon first, as it is easier to do when the fruit is intact.

Always, but always, use fresh organic unwaxed lemons whenever lemons are mentioned.

Always use sea salt and freshly ground black pepper unless otherwise stated.

All meat is free range and organic, all fish should come from sustainable sources.

WEIGHT

Imperial	Metric	Imperial	Metric	Imperial	Metric
½oz	10g	4oz	110g	10oz	275g
¾oz	20g	4½oz	125g	12oz	350g
1oz	25g	5oz	150g	1lb	450g
1½oz	40g	6oz	175g	1lb 8oz	700g
2oz	50g	7oz	200g	2lb	900g
2½oz	60g	8oz	225g	3lb	1·35kg
3oz	75g	9oz	250g		

DIMENSIONS

Imperial	Metric	Imperial	Metric	Imperial	Metric
⅛ inch	3mm	2½ inch	6cm	7½ inch	19cm
¼ inch	5mm	3 inch	7·5cm	8 inch	20cm
½ inch	1cm	3½ inch	9cm	9 inch	23cm
¾ inch	2cm	4 inch	10cm	9½ inch	24cm
1 inch	2·5cm	5 inch	13cm	10 inch	25·5cm
1¼ inch	3cm	5¼ inch	13·5cm	11 inch	28cm
1½ inch	4cm	6 inch	15cm	12 inch	30cm
1¾ inch	4·5cm	6½ inch	16cm		
2 inch	5cm	7 inch	18cm		

VOLUME

Imperial	Metric
2 fl oz	55ml
3 fl oz	75ml
5 fl oz (¼ pt)	150ml
10 fl oz	
(½ pt)	275ml
1 pint	570ml
1¼ pint	725ml
1¾ pint	1ltr
2 pint	1·2ltr
2½ pint	1·5ltr
4 pint	2·25ltr

OVEN TEMPERATURES

Gas Mark	°F	°C
1	275	140
2	300	150
3	325	170
4	350	180
5	375	190
6	400	200
7	425	220
8	450	230
9	475	240

AMERICAN CONVERSIONS

American		Imperial	Metric
1 cup	flour	5oz	150g
1 cup	caster sugar	8oz	225g
1 cup	brown sugar	6oz	175g
1 cup	butter	8oz	225g
1 cup	raisins/ sultanas	7oz	200g
1 cup	currants	5oz	150g
1 cup	ground almonds	4oz	110g
1 cup	golden syrup	12oz	350g
1 cup	uncooked rice	7oz	200g
1 cup	grated cheese	4oz	110g
1 stick	butter	4oz	110g

LIQUID CONVERSIONS

American	Imperial	Metric
1 tbsp	½ fl oz	15ml
⅛ cup	1 fl oz	30ml
¼ cup	2 fl oz	60ml
½ cup	4 fl oz	120ml
1 cup	8 fl oz	240ml
1 pint	16 fl oz	480ml

PARMUTO

First published in Great Britain in 2013 by Parmuto.
www.parmuto.com

Hardback ISBN   978 0 9574006 0 3
Paperback ISBN   978 0 9574006 1 0

Printed in the UK by Butler Tanner & Dennis Ltd

Art Directors: Yasemen Kaner-White, Aubrey Kurlansky
Designer: Matt Thom
Editors: Yasemen Kaner-White, Frances K White, Josephine Bacon

ACKNOWLEDGEMENTS

Where to begin? Many people in their own special way have contributed to *Lemon Compendium* and, of course, I would like to thank every single one of you. So, beginning with my forever supporting and encouraging Mum – thank you Mum, my amazing friends, loving family and even randomly met strangers who have enthused my writing and completion of this book – thank you sincerely for your support. Thank you to everyone who has shared their personal lemon stories, enriching beautifully the contents of the book. As regards producing, thank you to the fabulous photographers and a special thank you to Aubrey Kurlansky (Art Director) and Matt Thom (Designer) who have remained enthusiastic and a faithful 'second opinion' on tap – you guys are awesome, THANK YOU!!!

Thank you to all of the international lemon festivals who gave me their beautiful photographs to use (p.22–5) and another big thank you to the Michelin starred chefs who have both supported and contributed: Mauro Colagreco (Mirazur) Ernesto Iaccarino (Hotel Ristorante Don Alfonso 1890) and Giuseppe Aversa (Il Buco Ristorante).

MATT THOM

The page layout was designed by Matt Thom.
Matt is a graphic designer and photographer based in London. A graduate from Central Saint Martins who works in publishing, branding and print design.
www.matt-thom.co.uk

AUBREY KURLANSKY

Aubrey is a graphic designer, chef and fine-art photographer. He also runs a cooking school in London.
www.aubreykurlansky.co.uk
www.theheartofcooking.com

CREDITS

ILLUSTRATOR
Dorottya Kollo
6, 7, 28, 29, 30, 31, 36, 37, 38, 42, 43, 44, 45, 54, 55, 56, 57, 58, 59

PHOTOGRAPHERS
Aubrey Kurlansky
back cover, 9, 35, 39, 61, 111, 115, 122, 133, 141, 157, 167, 168, 176, 179, 186, 192, 195, 213, 227, 243, 245, 278

Ben Nankivell
249, 250, 252

Chinedu Okafor
201, 209

Chelsea Jacobsen
end papers, 17, 27, 73, 75, 76, 79, 81, 85, 88, 91, 92, 94, 139, 235, 263, 264, 271, 272

Chloe Smith
113, 119, 120, 127, 129, 130

Izzet Köroğlu
title page, book spine, 21, 41

Matt Thom
47, 53, 97, 99, 105, 107, 108

Mirazur
185

Il Buco Ristorante
205

Ennio Calice
207

PARMUTO